Publishers: Emily Schultz and Brian Joseph Davis
Senior Editors: Kevin Chong (Vancouver) Brian Joseph Davis (New York) Kara
Levy (San Francisco) David McGimpsey (Montreal & Atlantic) Charles McLeod
(Midwest) Emily Schultz (Toronto) Mathew Timmons (Los Angeles)
Web Developer: Ross Merriam
Editors Emeriti: Levi Stahl, Casey McKinney, Faye Guenther, Edward Gauvin, Wyatt
Williams, Janine Armin

Contact: joylandmagazine@gmail.com

Joyland Retro: Vol.1 No. 1, 2012
ISBN: 1468065599
ISBN-13: 978-1468065596

Cover art, "Thousand Plateaus-1914 N0 4," and design: Marc Ngui

# JOYLAND RETRO

## Vol 1 No 1

# CONTENTS

i

Joyland South

# FOR THE BENEFIT OF OTHERS
## Roxane Gay

Whenever my mother explains why she does things she resents having to do she says, *noblesse oblige*, nobility demands it. She tells me we have a certain responsibility. We must live up to it.

There are lots of benefits for Haiti in South Florida, hosted by tan, well-heeled people, most of whom have never visited the country. My husband and I are often invited to these events, always loosely named as "A Benefit for Haiti," or "Help for Haiti." We sit at round tables with cheap tablecloths and tropically themed centerpieces. We eat catered food. Sometimes the catered food is Caribbean inspired with dishes like jerk chicken or callaloo as if simply serving cuisine from the general region is enough to evoke the spirit of Haiti. I drink a lot at these benefits, sipping gin and tonics slowly from sweaty, tall glasses. I drink until I don't mind that reggae is playing when it is *konpa* we should hear. Whether the benefit is in Miami or Naples or Coral Gables, there is always a moment when the benefit's host stands behind a podium and smiles out at the audience with gleaming white teeth. They adopt a compassionate air and speak in clear but hushed tones about the problems of Haiti. They urge us to open our pocketbooks, to help, to build schools and feed orphans and provide desperately needed medicines. I love to look around the room during these impassioned pleas. I love to look at the white people with their shiny faces and linen outfits and expensive jewelry, how they nod and smile and pretend to care so they can feel better about themselves and their tax bracket.

The last benefit we attended was for the Mother of Mercy Orphanage in Cap Haitien. All around the banquet hall, there were huge, colorful pictures of skinny Haitian children with narrow necks and big heads. Most of the time, the children looked happy. As we walked around the room looking at the pictures of these orphaned

3

children, I said, "At least they don't have flies all over them like the African children," and my husband, Michael, sighed. He hates what he calls *my attitude*. I have a tendency to make judgments about everyone and everything based on incomplete information and casual observation. "Well, it's true," I said. He shook his head and took my hand and steered me toward the bar. As we stood in line, a tall blonde woman who always smelled like too much perfume swept through the crowd and made a beeline toward us. When she was a few feet away, she raised a well-manicured hand in the air, showing off a gorgeous diamond ring. Every wealthy woman in South Florida has a gorgeous diamond ring on her finger and several in reserve. She extended her hand even though we weren't close enough to reach. She said, "Murielle, it is such a pleasure to meet you again." I smiled and said, "Likewise." I turned to Michael. I could not remember her name but she was a regular on the benefit circuit. We also saw her at fundraisers for diabetes and cancer and heart disease. Her banquet-based beneficence knew no bounds.

Michael cleared his throat and squeezed my hand. "Jacqueline," he said. "It is a pleasure, as always."

I breathed a sigh of relief, and squeezed his hand back, leaning into him, sinking into the warmth of his shoulder. I promised myself to thank him later for doing what he always does—paying attention to the things I choose to ignore.

Later, after being entertained by the musical guest, a once famous R & B band now being kept together by an almost desperate desire to remain relevant, I excused myself from a conversation with a retired lawyer and a soon to retire plastic surgeon about malpractice and elective surgical procedures. I told Michael I would be right back and he said, "Hurry," because he knew I had no intention of doing so.

I sat in the bathroom stall listening to easy listening, Lionel Richie calling out to me, "Hello," over and over. I wanted to be the one Lionel Richie was looking for. I studied the patterns in the marble floor. The room spun slowly as the drunk I was nurturing settled in. When I knew I couldn't hide any longer, I exited the stall. Jacqueline was studying her reflection in the mirror, then she painted her lips with a fresh coat of dark red lipstick. She smiled at me. I nodded. She said, "You must have married into money."

I shook my head. I said, "No, he did." As I walked away, I noticed the reflection of Jacqueline's lips curled into a perfect, red, "O."

*Roxane Gay lives and writes in the Midwest but also spends a lot of time in South Florida. You can find her everywhere at* roxanegay.com.

New York

## CHAPMAN'S GREEN HAIRSTREAK
### James Greer

Even the sun runs late in Paris. In the pre-bloom dark, from an unshuttered window five stories above the street, Thomas Early could hear the Turks on the sidewalk arguing about attar of Damask rose. In Turkey the production of attar is strictly regulated by a state-run collective, but these guys were rogue producers, distilling in moist cellars the fragrant oil that had, in the past, both started wars and ended them.

But now the world was coming to a natural conclusion, so the arguments that drifted on currents of metropolitan air to Thomas Early's ears were not merely pointless (they had always been pointless) but distracting. He had work to do. He had to finish his manuscript. The ostensible subject of his manuscript was "The hardened sap, or gum resin, excreted from the wounds of the American Sweetgum," but the important part, the part that had to be finished before day's end, was a record of the last words spoken by Caeli Fax before she left for the countryside, where Thomas would join her when his work was finished.

Thomas turned away from the window and moved toward his desk, which was really a table, made of black alder (*Alnus glutinosa*) taken from the pilings of the now-collapsed Rialto in Venice and varnished dark brown. Before serving the Rialto the wood had been chopped from a copse in Clapham Commons and taken from there to Brighthelmston for use on its famous pier. But the pier, in fact a disappointed bridge, was already finished, so the wood was shipped to Italy. How it came to the atelier of Jakob Friedlander, *ébéniste*, in the 4eme arrondissement in Paris is a mystery, and possibly a scandal.

The table was piled with books and a confusion of manuscript pages, all covered in Thomas Early's tidy handwriting in black ink. He was wearing a dark blue polo shirt, short-sleeved, and black tennis shorts. His hair, cropped closely and without care, was dirty blonde. He was tall, 188 centimeters in his bare feet, and he was barefoot. His curiously ovoid face was covered in a week's worth of stubble, flecked with gray, and his small watery blue eyes were set back in their orbits, so that it was difficult to detect movement of corneas. His eyes had acuity of 50 cycles per degree, which gave Thomas an extraordinary ability to distinguish fine detail from long range.

The room was small, approximately five meters square; and on the floor lay a faded seventeenth century Persian rug of excellent design. The light from the table lamp spilled over into a silvery semicircle on the rug, revealing an intricate rosette pattern that, although Thomas did not know this, predicted with uncanny accuracy not just his future but all of his futures. The tightly woven wool fibers of the carpet comforted his feet the way a sweet caress will stop a lover's tears, in Norse mythology (see: *Helmskringla*).

We had always had hopes for Thomas Early. We had thought he'd be the one to stop the spread of World Fever, to find a cure, to save us. If anyone could, it would be him. We had not considered that, having found the cure, he would refuse to use it. That he would refuse to save us. Out of love. Out of the kind of over-whelming love that offers insight, that understands: the cure is not a cure.

The intervention of Caeli Fax proved crucial in this respect. She explained to Thomas Early the disastrous effects a plague of love would have on the human race; that far from mitigating World Fever it would in fact drastically increase the speed of its spread. Thomas was not easily persuaded, but because his mother had known Caeli's aunt in their shared hometown—Dayton, Ohio—he at first granted her his attention and after some time his trust. She brought him books: Burton's *Anatomy of Melancholy*; Blanchot's *L'arrêt de mort*; a biography of Salamander Pi. These were useful in his work, and too expensive for him to buy. She would arrive after midnight, and Thomas would light two fat candles (a gift from the Ecuadorian writer Charles Panic) that were now little more than hard pools of wax with furled edges impaled on the rusted wrought iron candle-stand (a gift from Oscar Delacroix). Thomas and Caeli often talked until dawn, or until Thomas fell asleep, at which time Caeli would slip out the window while Thomas drowsed, slumped in his leather club chair.

Caeli was slim, with delicate features, and graceful hands that she rarely used to emphasize a point. She would lay her left hand on Thomas' table, lightly drumming, and occasionally wave a lazy finger through the nearest candle's flame. Her right hand rested on her knee. Her large, long-lashed eyes, caramel brown with flecks of green, seemed black by candlelight, and sparkled when she talked, and sparkled more when she listened to Thomas talk. Most often she wore a tan trench coat over a blue cotton belted V-neck dress, and heavy leather boots with laces, though she would sometimes show up in old jeans with a white blouse, untucked. Thomas thought her very glamorous, precisely because she lacked any pretense to glamor. That she was not human only added to this perception. Her black hair was cut boyishly short, and she smiled often, which softened the angles of her pale face.

Her voice was light, especially in contrast to Thomas' rheumatic rasp, which for some reason had only deepened and thickened when he quit smoking, two years earlier. His septum had cracked in a snowball fight when he was eight years old, and never healed properly; as a result his nose was visibly crooked, and he had chronic rhinitis which, compounded by an allergy to dust mites, had eliminated seventy percent of his sense of smell.

—*If only one of those compacted globes of winter had not made contact with my face, at such a time, in such a way. Maybe now, all these years later, I would be able to breathe.*

—*If you could build a time machine, by which I mean another time machine, obviously, would you go back and dodge that calamitous ball?*

Most of the conversation between Thomas and Caeli was conducted in French, because they both felt more comfortable, or more at home, at least, in that language, though it was not their native tongue. "We are both exiles," Thomas had remarked, early on. "Everyone is an exile," said Caeli.

We had first begun to notice World Fever at the end of the last century, though at first we misunderstood both the symptoms and their underlying cause. When, a few years later, *Under An Azure Sky* (Expanded Edition with Notes) by Eddie Incognito was published, it was widely ignored. Thomas had been staying near Nice back then, looking for the soldier poet Gardner Stout, who was rumored to be living in an old farmhouse in a small hamlet somewhere in the neighboring countryside. He read *Under An Azure Sky* in one go sitting under the glossy leaves of a strawberry tree on the edge of a meadow and immediately recognized its importance. Within a decade, everything Incognito outlined in his book would come true. Within fifteen years, we would all be infected. World Fever is that powerful, that attractive; no one stood a chance. No on except Thomas Early. That, at least, was the hope.

Having finished the book, he put it aside and lay down in the shade of the small tree. He noticed a butterfly fluttering around the tree's hermaphrodite, bell-shaped white flowers, and recognized it as a Chapman's Green Hairstreak. Watching the little green imago, he realized that Gardner Stout must be very close. But he no longer cared.

That was probably a mistake, Thomas considered, sitting down at his table and shuffling some papers, looking for the heavily marked-up Wikipedia printout about the Rose of Castille. Gardner Stout had many bad qualities, but he would have recognized the importance of *Under An Azure Sky*. And unlike me, he would have done something about it. He would not have wasted his time undermining the Collective, or trying to find a publisher for his novel. These were both worthwhile pursuits, in themselves, and I'm not sorry I chose to do either, nor do I regret the time I spent on my two small volumes of poetry, but had I instead turned my attention to World Fever, I might not have proved such a disappointment to my friends.

The Collective had started out, as most things do, with good intentions. Literature was moribund. Books were not dying: writers were simply not writing anything anyone wanted to read. It was suggested that by pooling resources and ideas, a select group of the most talented young writers might come up with something fresh, something appealing, something that would enchant an entire generation of new readers.

Unfortunately, the select group of talented young writers could not agree on a new direction, a fresh angle. It could not agree, in the first place, on its membership. Who was talented? Who was not? What is talent? What is literature? What does it mean "to write"? What does it mean "to live"? What does it mean "to mean"? What does to what does what mean to what? And first of all, who?

The initial group was culled from a much larger group by a committee of older writers selected by another group of old men and women [that included writers, politicians, academics, journalists, critics, and (for the sake of inclusivity) schoolchildren, Catholic priests, Anabaptist ministers, Muslim clerics, vagrants, chimney sweeps, photographers, athletes from several sports, the wheelchair ping pong champion of Saint-Ours, a few circus freaks, a professional hypnotist, three psychiatrists, a man who could not pronounce the word "orange," a Freemason who denied he was a Freemason, which proves that he was a Freemason, a potter, a shoemaker, the CEO of a multinational bank headquartered in Paris and her husband, a bad painter, a very intelligent Labrador retriever, the head of the local Falconer's society, an imperious Nepalese woman from the tax department, a deaf and mute chess prodigy who communicated by spitting in Morse code, an ex-lion tamer, an artisanal AOC-rated goat cheese farmer, a troupe of mimes, an insurance salesman, a notoriously bad plumber, a leper, a giant sand crab, several species of fern, a barn swallow, a trained black bear, the ghost of Malcolm X, Jean-Luc Godard (who participated via Skype), the entire Swiss army, a Russian spy, and the Crown Prince of Sweden, all of whom were color-coded and ranked according to a complex rating system devised by a team of string theoreticians while walking toward (or away from) the Jardin des Plantes], all of whom had received their invitations by regular mail in unmarked envelopes, with the result that half the recipients simply threw their invitations into the trash, unopened. When the selection of older writers to select young writers of talent committee had achieved a quorum (there was a last minute panic that not enough Jews had been included, which received a strong objection from the grandson of an SS propaganda officer who had taken the Labrador retriever's place after shooting it in the head, but his objection was voted down, and he was beaten to death, after which three Hasidic men were coaxed from in front of the UGA Theater on the Champs Élysées), a vote was taken.

After the vote, over half of those elected to the Young Writers of Talent Committee declined to participate, necessitating three further rounds of voting until enough Young Writers of Talent could be convinced to form a committee and begin to formulate corrective measures designed to set a course for the drunken boat of contemporary fiction. Which is when the real trouble started.

One faction insisted that literature had become irrelevant to the lives of ordinary people, and that in order to remedy this, new work should strive not just to relate but to prove useful to the man or woman on the street. This was the Utilitarian Faction, to which Charles Panic belonged. Another faction stressed the importance of multiculturalism (the Pluralist Faction); still another pushed the notion that in order to engage, stories must excite the senses (the Satis-Faction). This last group was dismissed as pornographers, and quit the Collective in a huff.

The last, most powerful, and most secretive cadre of the Collective consisted of only five members, all of whom had joined with the aim of preventing the Collective from doing anything substantive. This faction called itself (albeit only among its members) the Anti-Collective Faction, or more informally the Antis. Meetings were held monthly in a small flat in Montreuil owned by Jérôme Soubeyrand, formerly president of the French Screenwriter's Guild, though he had left the movie business in disgust and vowed never to return "until they learn to respect the writer's work." Jérôme was a disheveled, professorial type with a graying beard and similarly graying, shoulder length hair. His flat was similarly disheveled. Books were piled on every available surface, with no sense of order or purpose. Dust balls the size of mice and mice the size of rats (because they were rats) roamed freely the few available avenues between the piles of books. You couldn't walk without tipping over a stack, which inevitably precipitated a chain of collapsing stacks that raised such a cloud of particles and waves you couldn't see, or breathe, or accurately measure the passage of time for some time.

Jérôme was very generous with his extensive wine cellar, and was always popping downstairs to retrieve this or that hand-labeled bottle of particular interest which he insisted on pairing with a specific cheese, also hand-labeled, or unlabeled, bought directly from some tiny cheesemaker in Brittany. He had very little money, but had managed to pay off the mortgage on the house, and what little he did make from sales of his books, or the occasional act of journalism, he spent on wine, cheese, and sausages that he would obsessively track down from the producer, wherever he or she might be situated. Thus every monthly meeting would begin late, and end later, and the next day no one could remember anything that was discussed, specifically, though everyone agreed that many things had been discussed, and with vehemence, and moreover that whoever had been tasked with taking notes had done an excellent job given the circumstances, and the fact that no one had remembered (or would admit to having remembered) to bring a pen. The thoroughness with which the Anti-Collective Faction accomplished absolutely nothing was taken as a grand success by its members.

Jérôme himself was a very fine writer. Not a major talent, but there were passages in, for example, *Plain Air*, that Thomas admired for their elegance of construction. Thomas had always found it puzzling that a writer capable of accessing the higher realms of his or her art did not do so always. Was it a question of not trying or inability? Once the imagination's unlocked, how do you stuff it back in its box? Or is it more like a current, that can be turned on and off with a switch, but sometimes you forget where the switch is, or you find a switch and flip it repeatedly but nothing happens, because it's the wrong switch? Perhaps certain people had the ability to tune out the radio air, to ignore the torrent of voices and noises sluicing down the wind, and thus withstand the impulse to document everything.

Thomas did not have that ability, and furthermore were he to develop that ability, it would leave him still with the problem of sight. The unparsed scumble of colors that narrowed into focus when he concentrated his unusually sharp eyes on a swath of sunlit carpet in his office; the many-hued sky; the dirt painstakingly collected under his fingernails: all these and more, much more, commanded Thomas Early's attention to the point where, in order to finish a job like the one currently under construction, he had to try not to listen, not to see. He didn't think his powers of concentration were inferior to others, but he was afraid of his powers of distraction.

Not everyone can carry the weight of the world. Only those born to do so, and even then only with proper training and a willingness to sacrifice, can make the merest attempt. The world is heavy, and getting heavier each day. Its borders are folding in on itself: the world is getting smaller every day. And the speed of things! Thomas had a great deal to say about the speed of things, but just at the moment he was in too great a hurry to elaborate.

He looked down at the paper on which he'd been writing in his smooth, almost calligraphic left-handed cursive. Picked it up in one hand, blowing lightly on the paper to dry the ink, even though the ink didn't need to be dried. An old and stupid habit, he thought. An affectation. When and where he'd picked it up he could not remember, but on the list of things Thomas disliked about himself, his habit of blowing dry the ink on a paper (which he did even when writing in pencil) was not even in the top one hundred. Nevertheless. It starts with the little things, he had been taught. A policy of tolerance toward skewed details will inevitably gather size and momentum until that policy comes to dominate the larger contours of your life: a *lapsus calami* becomes a *lapsus linguae*; and then life itself becomes one big lapsus, a descent into torpor where everything slides or is let slide by uncaring eyes.

Thomas had a horror of laziness, a physical repulsion at the thought of himself becoming lazy. In rare moments in between projects his limbs would seem to twitch, and his jaw clenched tight first on one side, then the other. He would knit his fingers together and wiggle them reflexively, neither church nor steeple nor see all the people but a squirmy sea creature yearning to break free from the ocean floor. He had refused to join any faction of the Collective in part because he feared that doing so would interfere with his work (which of course was the point of the Collective, so his fear in that respect was well-founded) and in part because he considered all but a very few of his peers extraordinarily lazy. When Jérôme asked him to join the Anti-Collective Faction, he had initially considered accepting, because the idea of interfering with the interferers appealed to him, but he began to suspect, even before their first meeting, that the Anti-Collective Faction was if anything lazier than any other faction, and further that their antagonistic pose was derived as much from apathy and arrogance as from as from any genuine alarm at the potential for harm resident in the very notion of a Collective.

He read again the words he had just finished writing down, the words spoken by Caeli Fax. A shudder passed though his neck on its way to the base of his spine as he read:

Darkness inside the muted light of sunset: when you stand in front of the window and stare at the far hills. These are the bad angels, gathering in gloomy bunches like poisonous grapes, parmite with blood. The leafless trees scratch with upstretched arms at scudding clouds, and in the growing mist barn owls perch on lower branches, scanning the radio air for the slow heartbeat of approaching doom. The bad angels grasp in their grasping claws the agenda of nightmares, larded with entrails of dead shrubs and bits of Styrofoam and brick. You roll the heavy door across its track and fasten tight the locks. You know that nothing made of something can stop the angels, who are nothing. You've looked them in the eye and seen the end of time, and the end of time was a mirror. And still you roll the door, and still you light the fat candle, and the wax drips forest green on polished marble floor: you turn and find yourself inside a tomb, which is where you keep the rain, for safety.

But you are not safe. The rain cannot keep you bright for long, and your tears will only fall, unseen. There are corridors in this place that lead to holy places, but all the holy places have been destroyed, out of love, out of a desire to love that burns without burning—a plague of love, a cholera of kindness. Dig a ditch and wait for pistol shot in back of neck. Or is that too romantic? Would you prefer a meaner death? Shriveling for years in the data basement, in an old hard drive, dispersing bit by bit on the ocean floor of knowledge, frozen, unexplored, blind, pressed flat by calamitous gravity.

Recursion is certainly the central metaphor for the text's operation. But we quickly see that precise repetition does not occur; rather, variation emerges, creating comedy.

I did not expect this sadness, thought Thomas, shuffling the papers into order. Nor this fear.

*James Greer is the author of the novels* Artificial Light *(LHotB/Akashic, 2006) and* The Failure *(Akashic, 2010), and the nonfiction book* Guided By Voices: A Brief History, *a biography of a band for which he played bass guitar. He's written or co-written movies for Lindsay Lohan, Jackie Chan, and Steven Soderbergh, among others. He is a contributing editor for the Los Angeles Review of Books.* jamesgreer.net

New York

## PANGAEA
### Jim Hanas

Jeanie stared into the drawer beside her bathroom sink at all the foil disks ringed by plastic teardrops, each teardrop containing a tiny pill. She pulled a disk from the drawer and placed it in the flesh-colored compact on the edge of the sink. She pressed one pill through the back of the foil and through the back of the compact, then looked into the mirror as she swallowed. Pivoting on one brown suede pump, she opened a second drawer. She was alarmed by the number of contact lenses she had accumulated, and by their variety. There were clear ones, and tinted ones, and ones that would make her eyes (naturally brown) seem icy blue, or evergreen, or eerie, steely grey. One pair, unopened like the rest, she was certain would make her look like a cat.

Jeanie returned to the first drawer and counted the disks. Fourteen. Enough birth control for one year, two months. That's when Jeanie realized she was planning to quit her job.

"I'm planning to quit my job," she announced to a friend over lunch, as both women maneuvered around the oily baby corns in their Pan-Pacific fajita salads.

She presented the evidence:

- the fourteen disks
- the icy blue, and evergreen, and steely grey contact lenses
- the lenses she was certain would make her look like a cat.

The friend had to admit she was right.

"You've been thinking about this for a long time," she said.

"I guess so," Jeanie said, staring into her bowl.

In fact she hadn't thought about it at all. Her stockpile had taken her completely by surprise, or nearly so—because obviously she had given it some thought. Or at least there had been thinking. Thinking had somehow taken place. This was how it happened. This was how it had happened with her friend Erin, and her friend Emily, and now everything made sense.

Standing in her doctor's office, a clock (somewhere) ticking.

"I'm going to need more pills. Can you do that?"

"What, are you opening a clinic?"

"I like to be prepared."

Thinking happening even then. Plans being made. 401Ks being mentally spent. Levels of contentment—both current and projected—being silently gauged. Jeanie felt betrayed.

She drummed her fingers next to her bowl of corns and counted one, two, three pelvic exams in the last six months. Yes. Her mind was made up.

Jeanie did not dislike her job as assistant director of point of purchase displays at Pangaea, provider of low-priced consumer cosmetics. She did not dislike it at all, and as she pulled into the parking lot the following morning, she couldn't quite summon the distaste that her newly excavated decision seemed to require. She didn't have an office, but her cubicle was quite the thing. Wedged into one corner of the fourth floor, it consisted of two authentic walls and two portable walls sturdy enough to support framed renderings of displays of which she was particularly proud. She had not one but two extra chairs facing her desk, which allowed her to convene small meetings. Beyond these, a low counter supported by one genuine wall held works-in-progress: three-dimensional dioramas involving clear plastic lipstick silos, eye pencils tethered to delicate silver chains, and mirrors embedded in Plexiglas adjacent to the slickened faces of various semi-supermodels.

She would miss this. She would miss the faces, and the lipstick silos, and the clever theft-proofing solutions. She would miss lurking behind one-way glass, picking at bagels and watching women play together like girls.

It's not like she didn't like her job. She did not dislike it. Yet often she found herself in a certain position. Things needed to be done, and she did them, although she often didn't want to, or felt like she didn't, or something. And sometimes things lingered, needing to be done but not getting done, and she waited, not doing them, secretly hoping that they would all of a sudden get done. She sat at her desk and did things other than the things that needed doing. She flipped through magazines, and visited websites, and read emails. Then, when she had finally settled down to work, she would remember a magazine she had been wanting to read or a website she had been meaning to visit, and then enough time had passed that maybe she had gotten new email, from whom she could not guess, but she would check anyway, and if there was something there she would read it, and, hey—what was this?—a voice mail, and after a long phone conversation with Erin or Emily, she would remember yet another magazine she wanted to read, or another website she wanted to visit, and she would want very much to lie down.

Still, Jeanie knew that the work would eventually get done. Not miraculously, as she hoped, but by her. She would do it. A deadline would loom and terror at the prospect of not having done the work would consume her, materializing in her mind as a giant boulder or a fiery asteroid, hurtling swiftly and steadily toward her. This terror would become excruciating in the way that only insubstantial pain can be.

But somehow, as if the terror had really been the pulling back of a pendulum (rather than either a hurtling boulder or an asteroid), she would surge forward, fighting tears—until after work, when they flowed—and the result, a Plexiglas representation of health and beauty, would take its place on the wall reserved for displays of which she was particularly proud.

Sometimes she did lie down.

She drove home in the late morning, or at lunch, or sometimes in the mid-afternoon. She checked into a motel near the office if the urge to lie down was too much (which it often was), and she would lie there and look at the ceiling and the smoke detector, and be glad she wasn't at work, and feel grateful that terror was levitating—slowly and evenly—off of her.

"How long have you been here?"

Jeanie looked up from a magazine to see Frank standing by her desk.

Frank, the head of sales, was rarely in the office and never for long. He usually didn't bother to take off his coat. When he was around, he could be seen through the door of his office: talking on the phone, his briefcase standing on end by his knees. He never smiled in the office and was possessed by a bitterness he seemed determined to spread.

"Do you like it here?" he asked, standing in the doorway of Jeanie's cube—coat on, back straight, briefcase hanging from one stiff arm.

"Sure," she said, poking at some papers on her desk.

"Really?" This was a game she had played with Frank before. That she had responded meant she had already lost. Jeanie imagined that Frank had a schedule—that he rotated around the floor on a weekly basis, reenacting this grim conversation.

Frank was probably fifty, although Jeanie suspected that his grey hair was misleading. He was on his second marriage and had been with the company a long time. Jeanie had caught him in an unguarded moment once, outside the ballroom at a company party. The double doors swung open and Frank and his wife—a sophisticated-looking redhead of an appropriate age—came sweeping through, hand in hand, leaving early. Smiling. He had seemed like a different person.

"And how do you like it, Frank?" Jeanie asked.

"Motherfuckers," Frank said.

"Sorry to hear that," she said.

And then he was gone. Jeanie grabbed her things and walked to the parking lot.


Jeanie's mind raced as she pawed through her closet. What to wear to a resignation? She had fallen asleep at her motel and slept until morning, waking in sweat and confusion to drive home in the morning sun, itchy from sleeping in her clothes. It had happened before.

Her closet was full of billowing silk shirts, and sheathlike two-piece numbers, and heels with straps waiting to brace her feet—crimped by years of ballet lessons—at stylish angles. There were other outfits as well: getups involving vinyl pants, and wool skirts, and skinny silk ties. Not costumes, exactly, but not exactly not costumes either. True, she felt like another person—really felt it, believed it herself—like a rocker, or an au pair, or George Sands when she wore the pants and skirts and the ties, but not so that anyone would notice. They would not notice that she, Jeanie, was looking at them from inside and far away.

It would have to be soon, though. The resignation. The terror was intensifying, the lying down becoming more frequent. Maybe today, she thought as she rubbed a vinyl seam between two fingers.

The rocker. Definitely.


"How long have you been here?"

Jeanie was interrupted as she checked her voice mail. She looked up to see Rachelle, who was not from a foreign country but had cultivated the idea that she might be. Her speech was so precise it sounded like a second language.

"How long have you been here?" Rachelle repeated, hovering in the gap between one of Jeanie's fake walls and one real, actual wall.

Jeanie stuffed the phone into its cradle.

"Today? How long have I been here today?"

"Yes. I came by earlier, and you weren't here."

Jeanie couldn't decide if Rachelle's question was really a question.

"I just got here. I had an appointment."

"There's a meeting."

Jeanie nodded until Rachelle vanished.

As Jeanie approached the conference room, she could tell something was wrong. All the desks on the fourth floor were empty and the conference room was full. Everyone was there. Jeanie asked an intern by the door what was going on.

"Excitement," the girl said, beaming.

Jeanie edged her way inside and found a spot next to Frank against the wall. She nudged him and whispered in his ear.

"What's going on?"

"Motherfuckers," he mumbled.

Rachelle's assistant, an efficient woman the same age as Rachelle, came in and announced to the room and to the triangular box in the middle of the conference table—"New York, are you there? Chicago, are you there?"—that Rachelle would arrive in a moment.

"The ax?" Jeanie whispered to Frank.

"Sure," he said.

Jeanie, like the intern, was excited. It was exciting. It might be bad news, but it wasn't nothing. It was action. Interns gathered with younger employees, basking in the toughness of adulthood. The couple from accounting whose affair was an open secret talked intensely, like their plane was going down and who cared who knew now. Jeanie closed her eyes. She felt terrible about it—hoping for the worst while everyone around her prayed for the best—but all Rachelle had to do was say her name.

Rachelle's assistant returned and spoke into the box at the center of the table.

"New York, are you there? Chicago, are you there?"

Voices answered and Rachelle's assistant left, returning in a moment with Rachelle and two men. Rachelle read from a sheet of paper, then one of the men stepped forward with the details. It had already happened. The people he named were not in the room. They were somewhere else, receiving bad news. She hadn't been in the running, Jeanie thought, as the man, whom she had never met but who was probably her superior, finished his statement. Everyone filed out of the conference room and collected in small pockets around the floor. Jeanie saw the couple from accounting with their coats on, leaving early and laughing.

Jeanie returned to her desk and opened a magazine. Again Rachelle appeared.

"How's that eyelash thing going?"

"Good." Jeanie nodded. "Good."

"Let me see something tomorrow."

Jeanie nodded.

"Are you alright?"

Jeanie nodded again.

"I hope you know what you're doing," Rachelle said, cocking her head, indicating something. Jeanie kept nodding until Rachelle vanished, then grabbed her things and headed to the parking lot.

As she pulled into the motel, Jeanie worried that she would not be able to resolve the eyelash thing by tomorrow, particularly not now that she was pulling into the parking lot of a motel, where—if experience were any guide—she would sleep until morning. In the front office, the clerk did not ask about her luggage.

As Jeanie stepped back into the afternoon sun and started toward her car—she always pulled it around back, just in case—she was shocked to see Frank, coming toward her from the far end of the parking lot. He walked perfectly erect, one tensed arm swinging his briefcase. He was looking away but soon would not be and Jeanie had only a second to decide what to do. She did nothing. She stood there, smiling slightly—like she'd been expecting him.

"Hey, Frank," she said, managing a wave.

"Hello," Frank said.

"Big project due tomorrow," Jeanie began. "The office is crazy and..."

"I've seen you here before," he said.

"Well," Jeanie stammered. "Sometimes it's easier to think when, you know..."

"What do you do?"

"Like I said…"

"I lie down," Frank said.

"Sometimes I lie down. Sure. The big beds. They can be hard to resist."

"That's all I do," Frank said. "I just lie down."

Jeanie nodded.

"Well, I better get to it," she said, checking her watch and waving her key card between them.

"Before somebody sees us?" Frank said.

Jeanie kept nodding.

"What will people think, right?"

Jeanie nodded until she realized what Frank meant. Is that what people thought? What Rachelle, and Erin, and Emily thought? Suddenly Jeanie did not feel well hidden in her vinyl pants.

"Because we're both always out," Frank said. "Because we're both always here."

"But Frank," Jeanie said. "I didn't even know."

"I know," he said, stepping past her into the front office.


On top of the bedspread, lights off, air-conditioning on full blast, Jeanie stared at the ceiling and the smoke detector, and waited for the terror to levitate off her, but it did not. It weighed, still and heavy. She pulled the chain that turned on the light and rummaged in the bedside table for stationery. Sitting cross-legged on the bed, the Yellow Pages on one knee for support, she began a letter.

*Dear Rachelle,*

*Did you know that Cuba used to be part of Florida? That Japan used to be a part of China? That the rivers, here in the middle of the country, didn't used to be here but were caused by complicated vectors of liquid, pressure, and temperature that could have scarcely emerged less than 10 million years ago? And that all of these will be compressed and/or expanded by the same forces from now until, I guess, forever. Ten million years from now, the world will be unrecognizable.*

*I have been stockpiling birth control and contact lenses. I am terrified. I want to lie down.*

Jeanie tore the letter from the pad, threw it on the carpet, and went into the bathroom to wash her face. Looking past her hands as she scooped water from the faucet, she caught herself in the mirror. And she did. She did look just like a cat.

*A native of northern Kentucky, Jim Hanas spent the '90s in Memphis, Tennessee, before moving to New York. His short stories have appeared in publications like* McSweeney's, One Story, Fence, *and* the Land-Grant College Review. *These and other stories are collected in* Why They Cried *(2010)—now available as a Joyland eBook from ECW Press. His nonfiction and humor pieces have appeared in dozens of publications, including* Slate, Salon, Print, Communication Arts, the New York Daily News, *and* the New York Post. jimhanas.com

Montreal & Atlantic

# I'M SORRY AND THANK YOU
## Andrew Hood

He came out onto his porch and there was some hippy mother changing her baby on his lawn. On a Hudson's Bay blanket, the mother was wiping and dabbing at the muddy rolls and creases of her little girl. A gust of wind whipped up leaves around the two, and it was like last night on TV. Some pear-shaped Spanish grandma had been crammed into this glass booth with money being blown all around her. The grandma grabbed at the bills, stuffed her clothes with money and wore twisted look of desperation on her face. She looked so stupid. He couldn't tell if the point was to degrade the grandma, but he could tell that this particular grandma didn't care. When the wind in the booth was turned off all the money dropped and lay in a pile at her feet. All that money just right there, but not for her. She had gotten some, but not enough. Never enough. The brittle and wet leaves stuck to the hippy mother's dreadlocks and onto the swamp of the little girl.

"I'll just be a sec," the hippy mom said when she saw him there on the porch. He took a sip from his mug and nodded, slid a hand into the pocket of his housecoat as a sign of being A-okay with things.

The hippy mother stood up with a bundle in her hand and walked to him. The baby writhed on the blanket like it was trying to crawl along the air.

"Hi," the hippy mother said. She had one of those cute faces that would have been ugly if she had tried to pretty it up with make-up, he thought.

"Morning," he said.

The mother winced at the sun high above them and looked back at him, squinting still.

"Listen," she said, "I'm sorry to do this, but I've got nowhere to toss this." She held up the bundle. "I was wondering if you wouldn't mind taking it for me."

"That's shit in there?" he asked, gesturing at the bundle with his mug.

"Pretty much."

"I don't know why," he said, "but I always think that babies have those things that birds have. Now, what are those things called?"

The hippy mother didn't know.

"You know. It's that thing that birds have where they do a combination of pooing and peeing so you can't tell what the hell it is that's coming out. It's called something, what they have. It's like "The Cloister," only it's not. It's right there." He shut his eyes tight and gritted his teeth, trying to force the word to the surface.

"Fuck," he said, popping open his eyes. "It's frustrating, huh? When you can't think of a word you know. It's like having one of those sneezes where you can't sneeze. Do you ever get those?"

The hippy mother did get those. She was smiling still, but it was a smile that didn't mean anything, like when a car in front of him would leave a turn signal on.

"Do you mind if I just leave this here?" she asked, and anyway bent down and set the soiled bundle on the bottom step of his porch.

"Just so long as you don't set it on fire," he said, and laughed.

"Right. I promise not to," she said. "But thank you. And, again, I'm sorry. She already... And I was just going to... Anyway, I'm sorry and thank you."

She turned and walked back across the lawn, picking leaves out of her hair.

"Don't forget your baby," he called from the porch. He took another sip from his mug and made a surprised, sour baby face, expecting it to actually be coffee, forgetting about the Canadian Club. The only club he'd ever belonged to, his wife used to say. She had thought she was just a riot, that woman. Now, there was someone he'd like to cram into a booth. But not a booth with money. Maybe a booth full of razor blades or something. How easily could those become airborne?

"Got her, thanks," the mother said, gathering up her squirming girl.

He watched her put the kid into one of those hippy slings that he was starting to see regular people use now, too, and he watched her go, watched her bum as she went.

"Cloaca," he said.

"Cloaca!" he yelled. "It was the cloaca!" he yelled at her. Down the sidewalk, the hippy mother turned to look at him, then turned away and moved off a bit more swiftly.

"Cloaca," he said, feeling good, feeling like he had sneezed that sneeze out, or like he had suffered water in his ear all day from a swim or something and finally it was trickling out now, all hot and amazing.

"Cloaca," he said.

He had come out for the paper when he saw the shitty baby on his lawn. Now he squatted and sorted through the rolls that had built up by his door and found the one with the most recent date. All these people had died somewhere because of something, he read.

He picked out the business section, shook it out as he stepped down the steps of his porch, fluffed the paper, and then spread it next to the bundle the hippy mother had left him. With his bare toe, he nudged the wad of cloth onto the paper and wrapped it up.

He breathed in. There was the sweet and pungent smell, the complicated scent of baby shit. Any smell you miss, even if it's a bad one, is a good one.

Wadding the newspaper and the cloth full of shit into a ball the size of a softball, he walked to the end of the driveway, and then he threw it. The wad landed with a light heaviness onto his neighbor across the street's roof.

Opening his nostrils and opening his lungs, he hoped for that autumn smell, but still it was baby stench. He smelt his hands, but it was not his hands. It was all over the air now, that baby smell.

Another whirl of wind came and tossed the salad of dead leaves on his lawn. The leaves flirted around him, and he began to grab at them. He snatched all he could out of the air, stuffing them into the pockets of his bathrobe, and then into his robe so they scratched his bare chest.

The wind died and he stood there with the heap at his feet, his pockets full and his chest bulky. A leaf had landed in his mug. He could drink around that

"Cloaca," he said, feeling pretty okay about himself.

*Andrew Hood wrote a book of short stories called* Pardon Our Monsters, *which won the Danuta Gleed Award for Canada's Best Debut Fiction Collection. His forthcoming collection is* The Cloaca.

Los Angeles

## CARLA
### Ben Loory

Carla wasn't a waitress, but she played one in the diner. What she really wanted to do was take photographs. She used to tell me all about it as I sat there at the counter, ordering dishes almost blindly, and trying to make her laugh.

Carla was very thin and very, very pretty, and her voice seemed to come from far away. I'd try to ask her out as she came back from the tables, but I could never seem to find the words to say.

Then one day Carla told me a story. A story a friend of hers had told her. She said that if you went out to a field and closed your eyes, and tried to walk straight, you'd actually go in circles.

In circles? I said. Why would that happen?

I frowned; it didn't make any sense.

I don't know, Carla said. It's something about the brain. Maybe one side is more powerful or something.

Oh, I said.

It seemed to make sense.

We should try it, I said. Bring your camera. You close your eyes and do your best to walk straight, and I'll take pictures and document it.

And Carla looked at me—kinda funny, I thought—but then she gave a smile and said yes. And in the morning I brought my car and we drove out to the country, found a field, and went and stood in the middle of it.

Close your eyes, I said, and I raised the camera.

And Carla looked at me and closed her eyes. And then she raised a hand, and she covered them to be sure, and then she took her first step forward.

I stood there with the camera, wondering which way she would turn—left or right—when something different happened. Carla didn't circle; instead, she seemed to stumble.

Then she collapsed and fell to the ground.

Carla! I cried.

And I dropped the camera, and I ran across the field as fast as I could.

I knelt by Carla's side. Her eyes were closed and still.

I couldn't even tell if she was breathing.

The ambulance came and took Carla to the hospital. They hooked her up to all these machines. There were bright lights and long tubes and doctors and nurses.

But no one would tell me anything.

For weeks and weeks, I sat there with Carla. She was in a coma; it went on and on. I sat there every night, in a chair by the window, just watching Carla's silent, sleeping form.

And as the time went by, I felt worse and worse. I knew that it was all my own fault. If I'd never taken her out there—to that pointless, stupid field—Carla would be all right; she'd be fine.

So I got back in the car and went out to find the field. It was harder to find this time around. The weeds had grown much taller, but finally there it was.

Carla's camera was lying in the grass.

I stood there in the field, in the spot where Carla had stood; I stood there with the camera in my hand. And then I closed my eyes and I stared into the dark, and then I took that first step forward.

I think that I was hoping I'd collapse like Carla had, lose consciousness, and wake up in her arms.

But that didn't happen; so I took another step.

I walked for an extremely long time.

In my head, I think I saw myself traveling in circles. I wondered if I was turning left or right. But I didn't peek at all; I just kept going on.

When I opened my eyes, I was at the hospital gates.

And so I went on back inside and up to Carla's room. And there she was, still sleeping in the bed. She looked so thin and fragile—-even more so than before.

She looked like she was wasting away.

And so I set the camera down and turned and went downstairs. In the basement, I found the hospital cafeteria. I turned on all the lights and I opened all the cabinets.

Then I started taking items down.

I'd never really cooked anything before that day. I don't know why. I'd always eaten out. But now there was a thing inside that seemed to open up; the knowledge seemed to flow into my hands.

And so I started cooking, and I cooked up a feast. I made steak and lobster, gooseberry pie. I made Baked Alaska, mango tarts, and a great big Jell-O mold.

Then I piled it all on a tray.

And when I got back to her room, Carla was awake. She was sitting there, propped up in bed. And she looked at me and smiled and then she raised the camera.


She put it to her eye.

Smile, she said.


*Ben Loory lives in Los Angeles, in a house on top of a hill. His fiction has appeared in* the New Yorker. *His book* Stories for Nighttime and Some *is available from Penguin Books.*

San Francisco

# SOMETHING MORE
## Erica Lorraine

Avery was a rapist, but that's not the first thing you'd notice about him. You might observe his pale skin or his glasses, the way the slender metallic frames highlighted his blue eyes. How his eyelashes brushed up against the glass. Or maybe his narrow, straight nose, and the way he was thoughtful when he listened; how he tipped his head to the side to regard the speaker. Every week when she saw him, Jackie noticed his long, white fingers and how he held each stem over the bucket, weighing it between his thumb and index before adding it to the bouquet.

Jackie always bought the most inexpensive flowers: irises or tulips, a few stems of gerbera daisies. After her purchase, she went straight home, sixteen blocks, to put them in water. She discovered that the flowers cast a kind of dignity on the small apartment. But on this day, when she spied Avery from a distance, handling a blush-colored carnation, Jackie decided that she wanted something more.

She hung back on the crowded street corner and concentrated on Avery's movements. He queried every flower before committing it to the bouquet. He held a white tea rose against the pale hydrangea and questioned a slim orchid before trimming its stem. Avery spun the bouquet in his hands and tucked sprays of hypericum and green berry mums up under the roses. Jackie inhaled deeply, but the scent of the flowers was interrupted by the dampness of the street and she left, without purchasing anything, and then, two blocks away, turned around and walked back to the stand. Avery was alone now, discharging water into the street and stacking the empty buckets.

Jackie stared at the flowers, weighing the price as Avery would weigh a stem, and he said, before she even asked, that he'd make her something special. She nodded. There was a gravity to his movement then. He spent a long time gazing at the buckets of flowers before tapping a single one. She waited while he gathered several long branches of violaceous delphinium. He moved around the stand and added mulberry-colored roses, blue hydrangea, and magenta lisianthus.

He named each flower for her, ending the litany with a double white freesia. It was a surprising bouquet.

Jackie fumbled with her purse, groped for her wallet. From the outside it looked like any other transaction.

After three months, Jackie moved into Avery's house with a box of books, two boxes of clothes, and one of dishes. She carried a cheery teapot in her arms. Avery borrowed his boss's van to move the four boxes eight blocks. Jackie unpacked. She found her things fit easily next to his.

When Avery was nineteen, he saw a woman on the city bus. Imagine him, uncherished—alone. It's not just a word, lonely. Lonely adds to solitary a suggestion of longing for companionship, while lonesome heightens the suggestion of sadness; forlorn and desolate are even more isolated. Avery hated the woman on the bus. She carried friendship, that fragile animal, but she withheld it from him.

He sat alone. He took off his glasses and pressed his hot forehead against the window. He tucked his fingers under his thighs. There were any number of approaches; countless words that he could use to communicate friendship. Gestures to demonstrate affinity. Avery was not stupid. He knew that there were just as many things he could do to cause her to recoil. He saw the distance between them and anticipated her rejection. He rolled his forehead against the cool glass, eyes closed. They were the only two on the bus.

Avery was just nineteen. He followed the woman every day for two weeks. Even when he promised himself he wouldn't, he did. Eventually he knew the consistency of the barkdust under the rhododendron across from her building. He knew her neighbor's standard poodle, Lily, and her habits. He knew the woman's skirts: the gay striped one, with pink and yellow and thin lines of pale blue; the straight, somber grey one, with a little slit in the back; the emerald green, identical to the grey. Every day the woman from the bus rejected him in a thousand tiny gestures. She refused to meet his eyes.

One day, though, she saw him. She reported him. And he was caught under the rhododendron by two large police officers.

When Avery was young he was arrested for following the woman on the bus. Is that all that happened? That's all that Avery told Jackie.

When Avery was sick, Jackie was at her best. She loved to hold his face in both hands and slide her thumbs over his forehead until he closed his eyes, and the ropes in his neck loosened against the pillow. She wore a faded calico apron with lavender ricrac and wide pockets. She knelt next to their mattress on the floor and held Avery back against the sheets—he hated to stay in bed. The wind blew straight through the house. She wore the apron over an old sweater, a turtleneck, and a pair of corduroy pants. She wore two pairs of socks.

She kept him, naked and sweating, under every wool blanket and down comforter they owned, and fed him soup that she made from rendered chicken fat, yellow onion, and mashed cloves of garlic. Avery was as small as a woman. His thin, white skin barely covered the irregular pattern of beating blue veins. She stroked the inside of his arms and convinced him to lie still. Jackie believed she could cure him—it took attention. She stayed home from work, stayed home from school, and when his fever broke, she made him hard in her hands and fit herself on top of him. She held his wrists above his head and buried her face against his neck.

Jackie was good at a great many things and empathy was one of them. Avery trusted her. Bits of Avery's story leaked out over their years together. Even the uglier bits inspired compassion in Jackie.

But there was something about the borrowed van and the sick mother. Did he borrow the van at night, when Jackie was at class, to visit his mother? Avery's mother was very sick, this was true. And Avery's boss was quite generous about the van. Let's take a vacation in the van, Jackie suggested. But Avery didn't want to.

The greatest problem was the wood stove. Who had a wood stove in the city? Avery did, in his old house, and it was a perverse beast. Bad tempered, changeable. At first it was all very romantic: the forest-green living room heated by the fat-bellied stove. But she never mastered it. For kindling, they used lath from the empty attic. It was thin and musty and gave her splinters. She kept a pair of tweezers in the pocket of her apron. Avery had a sense, could get it lit, keep it lit, and use half the paper and kindling that Jackie did.

It was always winter. It raged on or crept through for months. Ice storms lacquered the city. Jackie was forever cold in the decrepit house.

But she loved to fill the mason jars with the day-old flowers he brought her: bruised freesia, cut violets, lilies of the valley. She cherished every drooping, engorged blossom. She went to work. She went to school. She brought stacks of wood in from the side of the house. When the city hit record lows, she got pregnant and Avery had to borrow the van from his boss to take Jackie to the clinic. Be careful, his boss said: There was black ice on the roads.

The abortion came out like a sneeze. Avery took her home and made them mugs of hot chocolate. Jackie tucked her legs up under her and accepted the blanket that Avery brought. She felt dreamy and drowsy. Avery stoked the fire and the forest-green living room crackled with heat. He sat cross-legged next to her and stroked the back of her hands with the tips of his fingers. It was strange how the abortion made them a family.


It's not that she was uncurious. Avery had shown her the box when she first moved in. He held her by the fingertips with one hand and touched the corner of the box with the other. It was more a chest, like a sea chest, than a box, but Avery called it a box and inside it held things that were meaningful to him. Mementos. His lips were dry and thin and they stuck together on the Ms when he said the word. Mementos.

Jackie was understanding. Above all, Jackie understood. And what she couldn't understand she could imagine. She imagined Avery's comfort and his hurt twisted together. For many months she didn't think of the box at all, and when she did, she was struck by an image of the lath from the attic, the violet-tipped flame it made. When she imagined what was in the box, she pictured this: a bright, blue flame. It wasn't that she was incurious, but that she understood.

They'd lived together for more than two years when she first opened the box—that unlocked chamber. And she no more expected to find him there than in the despoiled flowers. The box swung open for her. Its contents were not terribly surprising.


Avery turned the van down a familiar street. There, on the left, was the house where the woman lived. He parked and a moment later was standing in the bedroom of her house. The smell of her was stronger here. He knew her, had studied her for many days. How many days?

He pulled the curtains so that no one could see him inside, but the fabric was thin and the late afternoon light brightened the room. The walls were painted a sunny, lemony color and the woman had made her bed, her nightgown folded, resting on the corner. He was not a thief. He didn't go through her drawers.

He waited on the corner of the bed, not disturbing the carefully folded nightgown. As the room grew darker, Avery became angrier. He was tired of waiting. He stood up and with one movement struck out and broke a bedside lamp. It was porcelain and it shattered. Then Avery sat back down. He felt calm again. He could wait.

When the woman got home, she didn't notice the broken window, the closed curtains, Avery's proximity. She tapped on lights and then a radio and took off her jacket as she walked toward the back bedroom. When she saw Avery, she didn't notice any of the good things about him. She didn't take in his aquiline nose, his high cheekbones or the way his long lashes crimped under the small glasses. She didn't see the roughness of his hands or understand how hard he worked. She didn't consider how long she'd made him wait.

Five days a week Avery stood outside at the flower stand. He returned home with cracked, chapped hands and stiff, swollen fingers and Jackie washed them with a warm cloth. She smoothed on a thick, sticky balm. When he complained, she covered his mouth with hers and moved one hand down to unbutton his pants. Sex is your answer to everything, he argued, but he couldn't push her away with his sticky hands.

The cops came.

Avery was still at work, and when Jackie answered the door, she understood. The word "appreciate" would involve valuing or sympathizing with the information. Without value or sympathy, there is only recognition.

One cop sat on the forest-green couch and wrote in a little notebook while the other explained. They were confident that it was Avery. They had, in addition to the woman's testimony, placed the florist's van outside the apartment. They suspected him in other attacks. Other rapes.

Jackie listened as they described the victim. She pictured angry waves of dark yellow and streaky green bruises. Crimson scars. She thought of Avery's calloused, cracking hands with their beating blue veins.

As he spoke, the policeman fondled the edge of an overblown rose in a vase on the windowsill. Jackie stared at flower. Avery will be home any minute, she said.

Avery was late leaving work. He stacked the buckets, emptying water into the street. The remaining flowers were loaded onto a cart so they could be refrigerated overnight. As he broke down the stand and loaded the cart, he brushed an Asiatic lily and stained his sleeve with the powdery yellow pollen. He slowed and thought about Jackie. She never liked lilies; they reminded her of funerals, but these were so beautiful, not the common oriental hybrid.

Avery removed five stems from the bunch and gathered them loosely in one hand. He fished out seven stems of solidago and fit them between the bright red petals. He added three strong stems of Israeli ruscus. The scissors were in his apron and he trimmed the stems, but left them long. It was a tall, sunny bouquet.

*Erica Lorraine studied at Naropa University in the late 1980s and recently received an MA in creative writing at University of California, Davis. Her work appears in* Bombay Gin, Friction 9, *and* Rumble. *Her website is* royalquietdeluxe.blogspot.com

Joyland South

# JENNY SUGAR
## Scott McClanahan

When I was in the fourth grade this little girl in my class got killed. I showed up at school one Monday morning and Randy Doogan was telling me all about it, "Hey Scott did you hear about Jenny Sugar? She got killed in a car crash yesterday. Yeah a tractor trailer hit her Mom's car and they're both dead."

Of course, I didn't believe him at first because Randy Doogan was always making stuff up like this. He was always going on about how his Dad lived in England, even though this was just something his Mother told him because his Dad left them and never came back.

But he just kept going on about it. "Yeah my Mom saw it on the news last night and she's dead."

Then he giggled and moved on to the next kids sitting at the cafeteria tables, "Hey guys did you hear about Jenny Sugar and her mom? They got killed yesterday?"

I stood and giggled too not really knowing what was going on and wondering if it was true or not.

But it was true all right. We found out just a couple minutes later from our fourth grade teacher, Mrs. Morgan. She stood in front of our class and told us that Jenny and her Mother had been visiting Jenny's grandma in Virginia. On the way back home Jenny's Mom was driving behind this tractor trailer. Jenny's Mom was passing it on the right hand side of the road, but as she was passing it the truck pulled over and the car crashed beneath the truck. The poor driver kept driving because he didn't know what happened.
The tractor trailer driver drove for another five minutes before he finally realized he was dragging a car beneath him.

So after telling us this, Mrs. Morgan sat down at her desk and put her head in her hands. We were supposed to be working on our spelling words like "F-R-I-E-N-D-S" and "M-O-T-H-E-R" but everybody just stopped and watched her. She sat for a second and then she started to cry. It wasn't your typical sad cry now, but it was a cry that sounded different.

It was a cry a woman would cry if she wasn't our teacher Mrs. Morgan anymore, but a thirty-five-year-old woman named Elaine.

I put my pencil down and listened to her cry and thought, "Yes. Hallelujah! We're not gonna have to do any work today!"

Then another girl named Ammie started crying too. So Mrs. Morgan walked over and asked her if she needed to go to the bathroom.

Ammie nodded her head yeah.


Mrs. Morgan touched Ammie's shoulder and asked Nicole to go to the bathroom with her.

I leaned over and told my friend Mike, "What's up with that? She didn't even know her that well."

But inside my head I was just jealous because I wished I could be free too.


Finally Mrs. Morgan was able to compose herself and told us all, "I know this is a horrible accident but there is going to be a funeral tomorrow and I hope we can all go. I have permission forms you need your parents to sign tonight if you wish to go. I'll also be calling each of your parents tonight."

She said if it was too much for anyone, we could just stay behind and Mrs. Crookshanks would be showing a movie. Somebody raised their hand and asked, "What movie?" Mrs. Morgan said she didn't know. She thought maybe a Superman movie.

I didn't say anything but I was thinking—

Superman or the funeral?

Superman or the funeral?

I picked the Superman movie.

The next day at school it seemed like everybody else picked the funeral. Dumb bastards. They got on the bus all dressed up in their nice shirts and ties and church dresses and church shoes. We watched from the window as they got on the school bus and took off.

There were only a couple of us who didn't go that day. There was me, and Debra the retarded girl. And there was Kevin Van Meter, the kid who always pooped his pants. He wanted to go too, but since he always pooped his pants the teacher just made up an excuse so he couldn't go.

After they all left, we sat down in the dark classroom and Mrs. Crookshanks put *Superman IV* in the VCR. I sat and watched and there was a part of me saying: "This is great. This is two days in a row we haven't had to do any work. I mean who'd go off to a dumb funeral when there's Superman playing?"

But after only watching a half hour of *Superman IV*, I realized something important.

*Superman IV* sucked. *Superman IV* really sucked.

I mean you could see the wires that were holding Christopher Reeve up in the air, and the microphone was showing in one shot. Then all of the sudden Debra, the retarded girl, started crying. I was like, "Debra, shhh, or they're going to turn off the movie." So she finally quit crying. But *Superman IV* wasn't getting any better and to make matters worse I started smelling something.

I sniffed my nose a couple of times and then I turned to Kevin Van Meter and told him, "You pooped your pants didn't you?"

Kevin Van Metter kept looking at *Superman IV* and said, "No I didn't."

"Yes you did."

"No I didn't."

"Yes you did. I can smell it. You crapped your pants like you always do. It's no wonder they wouldn't let you go the funeral." Finally Kevin Van Meter raised his hand and did what he always did. He raised his hand and said in his deep, speech impediment voice, "I'm telling teacher on you."

The teacher came over and Kevin told her, "Teacher, he's picking on me."

But Mrs. Crookshanks smelled him too and instead of yelling at me, she just turned off the VCR and took Kevin to the bathroom. Shit. We didn't even get to watch the end of the movie.

It wasn't an hour later the school bus pulled back up in front of the school and they were back. They were all dressed up in shirts and ties, and nice dresses and for some reason or other they didn't look happy. I mean I even tried telling my best friend Matt Chapman about how *Superman IV* sucked and how he should be happy he went to the funeral.

"I mean, Matt, it was horrible," I said as he looked away from me. I laughed. "I mean you could actually see the cables holding him up in a couple of shots."

But Matt didn't say anything to me.

He just looked at me all disgusted.

I said, "How come you're acting like this and not saying anything?"

Matt shook his head and said, "I just came back from a funeral Scott. I don't care about some stupid movie that my Mom can rent for me down at Country Boys. And how come you didn't go? What's wrong with you?"

I thought, "What do you mean why didn't I go?" But then he gave me a look I'd never seen before. It was a look like my Dad gave me. It was a grown-up look.

For the rest of the day I sat at my desk thinking about how *Superman IV* sucked and then I started thinking about Jenny Sugar.

I thought about how a couple of weeks earlier my mother took a picture of her at a school carnival and she didn't smile. She didn't smile because she was embarrassed.

She was embarrassed because she'd just started wearing braces. I thought about the last time I saw her. We were both outside cleaning out our fourth grade lockers and I was trying to make her laugh by doing a funny voice.

"Hee hee," I laughed in my funny voice, but she didn't laugh. "Maybe she didn't hear me," I thought.

So I did it again, "Hee hee."

She just rolled her eyes, and shook her head, and went "Ugghhh" like I was so immature.

Maybe I was.

But over the next couple of weeks it was like the rest of the kids completely forgot about Jenny Sugar. It was like they were the ones who stayed behind and watched Superman instead of saying goodbye. It was like it never even happened. It wasn't even a week later and they were all laughing again, and doing fart jokes and playing touch football at recess.

I kept asking, "Isn't it strange that Jenny's gone? What was the funeral like? Were people crying?"

They acted like they didn't even know what I was talking about. And then one day doing my spelling words I came across a word.

It was spelled, "S-K-E-L-E-T-O-N." Skeleton.

So I stopped doing them. I looked around and all the other kids were spelling "S-K-E-L-E-T-O-N" like there was nothing wrong with it.

I went to the bathroom and passed two teachers in the hallway talking about Jenny's death.

They said, "I think they're holding up pretty well. It's just so horrible what happened." And then the other teacher whispered like she didn't want anyone to hear, "Well you can't even imagine it. I heard the little girl was decapitated and that's why they had a closed coffin. Imagine the father losing his wife and only child in the same day. I know he quit drinking when she was born. I wonder what will happen to him now?"

I kept thinking about it though.

I thought about Jenny Sugar without her head.

I thought about closed caskets.

I thought about Jenny Sugar's skeleton and blood.

Each morning I woke up and my stomach was hurting. I was in the bathroom so much my Mom started getting worried.

"Are you okay in there Scott?" she asked through the door.

"Yeah I'm fine," I said. "My belly's just a little upset."

"You want me to get you some more Pepto?"

I said, "Yes, Mam," but I kept thinking about it.

I thought about it so much that by the time school was over that summer I couldn't even get into my Mother's car. My Mom and I were supposed to visit my Grandma in Virginia, but I was dreading it. I hung out all summer getting even more scared, drinking Pepto-Bismol, worrying about how I wasn't baptized yet, and wondering how I was going to tell her I didn't want to go. I didn't want to go anywhere. I didn't want to get in a car and get killed by a tractor trailer. I didn't want to get decapitated.

This went on for weeks.

Then on the day we were supposed to leave I just sat in the car and I told her, "I don't want to go Mom. I really don't want to go."

And at first my Mom was mad, "Scott we're supposed to be leaving. Why didn't you tell me this a couple of weeks ago?"

Then it dawned on her that I was afraid. I was afraid something was going to happen to us.

I sat in the car and cried, "Why did Jenny have to get killed that way and lose her head?"

She shrugged and said, "I don't know."

I asked, "Where is she now Mom?"

She said, "I don't know Scott. I really don't know."

She was telling the truth. I was shaking now.

I said, "I don't want to go because I don't want something bad to happen to us. I don't want to be a skeleton."

My Mom thought for a second and said, "Nothing bad is going to happen to us. I won't let anything happen to you. There's nothing going to happen to us. I won't let it happen to us. I promise."

I was feeling better.

And then she said it again as we pulled away, "Don't you worry about that now. We're not going to get killed. There's nothing bad *ever* going to happen to us. I won't let it happen."

I wasn't crying anymore. My mother was a fucking liar.

*Scott McClanahan is the author of* Stories *and* Stories II *(published by Six Gallery Press). His other works include* Hillbilly, Stories V!, The Nightmares *and* Crapalachia. *His website is hollerpresents.com.*

Vancouver

# KINDLING
## Nathan Sellyn

When I went to meet Alison down on Granville Island, her brother Adam had been dead for two days. It was the end of September, but not raining, so I walked. I'd just moved into a studio in Yaletown, was trying to live the dream a little. When I got across the bridge and down to the Seawall I lit a cigarette, then ran the flame from the lighter back and forth across my palm. It took a few passes before my skin began to burn, before I found something Adam and I had in common.

It took me a few minutes to find her. She was drawn up against a bench behind the Public Market, sitting toward the water. It was obvious that she hadn't slept in awhile—hair lay in clumps against her forehead, and dried blood filled the cracks in her lips. An old UBC hoodie bagged over her shoulders, her knees and arms tucked up inside its chest.

She was facing away from me, staring at the traffic stumbling across the Burrard Street Bridge. If I surprised her, she didn't show it. Just turned and smiled a little, then leaned into my chest. I hugged her, knees and all.

*Hey Ali*, I whispered into her neck.

*Hey*, she said. *Thanks for coming.*

I hadn't seen her since we'd broken up, back at the beginning of the summer. But she had called that morning and wondered if I could meet, if we could talk a little. It was a Monday, but I told her sure thing and then called in sick. She didn't ask if I knew, because of course I did. Everyone did. Leah and Carl and Rich had all called me the morning after—*Holy shit, did you hear about Adam?*—and by that afternoon Janice and Mickey and Pauline had too. Death makes good gossip. No one had spoken to Alison, though. I was the first.

But I didn't know what to say. Didn't want to ask how she was doing, because there was only one answer. Didn't know if she'd even want to talk about it, figured maybe she was just looking to pretend things were normal for half an hour. Poor girl had probably been doing nothing but talking—to cops, to reporters, to family. Maybe she just wanted a break, an hour's vacation from the hysteria. I didn't know. Serious conversations were new territory for us. Even at its height, our relationship had been flimsy, its issues merely social—which restaurant, which bar, which friends we'd bring along. And when I'd broken things off I'd been surprised by how hard she took it, by how much she'd cried.

So I just squeezed her and didn't say anything. Her breath was stale. After a minute she pulled back and asked how I was doing, how my summer had been. I answered carefully. Didn't mention that I was still seeing the girl I'd left her for, or how well things were going at the new job. Only that I'd had a good few months, how I'd gone back to Toronto for a week to see my parents. That made her smile.

*How's your Dad?* she said.

*Good,* I said. *He still wants me back home. Thinks I'm just wasting time out here. You know how he is. Thinks Vancouver's still all hippies and retirees.*

She nodded. Two Japanese tourists stood a few feet away from us, their heads hidden beneath matching aviators and Tilley hats. They were taking pictures of each other in the shadow of the bridge. One of them took a few steps toward me, like he was going to ask for a shot of them together, but when he got close enough to see Alison he did a little gesture with his hands and backed off.

*You want a coffee or something?* I asked.

*No,* she said. *I'm fine. I'm sorry, I know this is random. I just... he liked you, Eric. More than any other guy I've ever dated. And you're not a very good listener, I know. But you always looked like you were listening. So... just sit with me for a while. Please?*

*Yeah,* I said. No problem.

She curled into me again and I put my arm around her. He'd liked me. It felt strange to hear that. I'd liked him too. How he always carried an umbrella. Told me once that he wanted to start his own umbrella company, making umbrellas for men, with wooden handles and cool patterns—skulls, dice, crowns, that kind of thing. I told him it was a good idea. That I'd buy one of those umbrellas.

*I was there,* she said. *Did you know that? I was, like, ten feet away.*

*Jesus,* I said. *That's... Ali, I'm so sorry.*

*No, it was good. I'm glad I was there. I don't think I'd believe it otherwise. You guys were at Plush, right?*

*Yeah,* she said. *Tim's birthday. Their cousin.*

*Was he on anything?*

*No.* She shook her head. *I was, but, you know Adam... he never. That's not his thing. Never needed it.* She was right, the kid had always been high energy. It was the first thing I noticed about him, even though he was only sixteen or so then, long before Alison and I got together. A party at her house, and she wasn't letting him drink, but he didn't let that stop him. He'd walked right up and introduced himself: Asked how I knew Alison, if I wanted some gum, where I'd gone to high school, what I drove, if there was a song I wanted to hear. Sometimes he'd be on another question before I'd answered the last one, like his mouth had been set on fast forward.

*Actually,* she said, *he was really quiet. Wouldn't leave our booth, not really talking to anyone but me. And he was sweating a lot. It was dripping off him. He was all paranoid over these girls he'd brought, really worried that they weren't having fun. And nervous. Kept spilling his beer.*

*Who were the girls?* I asked.

*I dunno, I'd never met them before. Just Surrey girls, nothing special. I think he knew them from BCIT. Anyway, by the end of the night he was pretty drunk, and he said he was going the washroom and I didn't see him for a while. I actually started to think he'd left. But I finally found him at the center of the dance floor, right in the middle of these girls. Then he was his old self again, all over the place, trying to do a waltz with one of them. I was staring right at him. It looked like he was singing. And then he started to smoke.*

*You saw it happening?*

*Yeah. I thought maybe it was steam, because he'd been so sweaty. But then there was more of it, and all of a sudden his hands were on fire, and I realized he wasn't singing, he was screaming, but... the flames went up his arms, and then everyone was screaming, there was this big crowd around him, like around a fight. And he tried to run off the dance floor, everyone moved to let him go, but when he got to the edge he fell down, his legs were on fire too, and then his hair. He was rolling around, trying to put it out, screaming and screaming and screaming. And then one of the bouncers got to him with a fire extinguisher, sprayed him all over. But it was too late... the heat must have been inside him, too. And the smell... people started throwing up. I ran over, but they wouldn't let anyone near him. His skin, his face...* She trailed off and closed her eyes, rocking back and forth inside her hoodie's tent.

*Ali, I...*

*I know,* she said. *If I wasn't there I wouldn't believe it either. My parents want to sue the club, they think it must have been the temperature inside or something like that.*

*What do you think?*

*I dunno. The doctors said it's happened before. That it's not impossible, just unexplainable. But there are records, I guess. Still, they can't say why. It doesn't make a difference.* She opened her eyes. She wasn't crying, but her skin had gone very white, pale enough to make out all the veins on her face. And I hoped my listening was helping, because otherwise I was useless. I had no idea what she was feeling. And I felt ashamed that I was the one she'd called, that I was the best she had.

*I went back*, she said suddenly. *Last night.*

*To Plush?* I asked.

*Yeah. My parents invited over all this family, uncles and aunts I haven't seen for years, and I just wanted to get out, so I went back. To Plush. I needed to. But... it was like it never happened. They'd cleaned everything up, the same music was on. Even some of the same people were there.*

*Jesus,* I said.

*And I heard these two girls talking about it. One girl was saying she'd heard some guy had died there the night before, how he'd just... exploded. And the other girl goes, 'Oh my god.' And that was it.*

We didn't say anything for a long time after that. I pulled another cigarette out, but as I patted my pockets for my lighter I changed my mind. A wind came up off the water, delivering a chill that crawled inside my sweater, made me shiver.

*I can't imagine it,* I said. *The not understanding.*

*That's not the worst part,* she said. *I mean...* She gestured toward another bench, where a chubby guy was barking into a cell phone. *I don't understand how that works, really. How the Internet works. Fuck, I don't understand how my birth control works, when I think about it. So... that's not so bad. But... what's hard is that I feel like it must mean something. There has to be a reason. Why it happened to him, I mean. I don't know what, thought. Was he special? Am I, maybe? I don't know...* She leaned into me again. *I just feel as if this can't happen alone. Something has to come next.*

And that was it. She was finished talking. We sat there for another twenty minutes or so, not saying anything, and then she got up and said she'd let me know about the funeral. I asked if she wanted help getting home, and she smiled and said she'd be fine, that she appreciated me coming. And then she left, toward the Market. I watched until her hoodie melted into the crowd.

As I walked home I thought about her going back to the club, listening to those girls. I thought about the nameless millions of other people—the ones who didn't know Alison, who hadn't known Adam. I imagined them leaning down for the paper outside their hotel room door, sitting with their takeout in front of the news, loading up their web browser. How for them the whole thing would just be one line – "Teenager bursts into flames at Vancouver bar"- and then they'd turn the page, chalk it up as one more little piece of crazy in this city.

The wind was still going strong, and at the edge of the island I hid behind a tree to light a cigarette. The leaves had just begun to turn, and there were golden freckles in their green. I wondered, for a moment, how nature decides which leaf falls first. Not that it makes a difference, of course. They would all be gone by winter.

*Nathan Sellyn is the author of* Indigenous Beasts, *published by Raincoast Books in Canada and Albin Michel in France.* Indigenous Beasts *was the winner of the Danuta Gleed Award for Canada's Best Debut Fiction Collection and shortlisted for the Commonwealth First Book Prize and the ReLit Prize.*

Midwest

## BABIES
## Ricco Siasoco

More incredible things had happened, Hugo thought, than a man giving birth. Frogs were born with six limbs; praying mantises laid eggs in gummy lines, backtracked, and then ate them like licorice. It was the last late afternoon of summer and Hugo propped his pillow up in bed, copyediting a piece about the equinox.

"I want to get pregnant," Hugo said, placing his hand idly on Mitchell's head. Earlier that day, in the crowded newsroom, a freckled intern had seen a push-pinned photo of him and Mitchell, and remarked that they would have the most beautiful children.

Mitch pushed Hugo's hand away. "You're kidding, right?" He placed his thin spectacles on a stack of milk crates—Hugo's idea of a night table. "Reality to Planet Hugo? We can barely pay our mortgage and now you want a child?"

Did the serious ever laugh? Mitch slid off the bed and removed his sweatpants. Hugo's boyfriend liked to worry about the quotidian things in life, repainting the bricks of their crumbling brownstone or toning his svelte, thirty-four-year-old body. Mitch was a freelance nutritionist. *Health,* he liked to repeat to Hugo, *was nobler than science. Your body is a temple.* Hugo outwardly agreed, keeping to himself the knowledge that biology was fundamental to Mitch's vain world of nutrition.

Science, on the other hand, was Hugo's bread and butter. He lay against their headboard and smoothed the velvety nap of the blanket. It wasn't child rearing or adoption Hugo craved (he hadn't thought that far ahead), but the actual creation of human life. His and Mitch's baby! He laughed, lifting his papers and imagining a baby with Mitch's pepper-gray hair and his own straw-colored skin.

Mitch locked in his plastic mouthguard and closed his eyes. In a minute he was snoring. Hugo set his papers aside and watched his boyfriend sleep, and then turned off his lamp. He lay motionless on his back, feeling the leafy shadows from outside shimmer on the painted walls. The room was like a giant aquarium. Slowly the blanket floated off him, billowing in the room of blue-black water. He too floated up from the bed, reaching his hands to his neck and touching the flaky gills beneath his chin. Light waves splashed the stucco ceiling, and a few fathoms below, Hugo could see the black silt collecting on his computer monitor and along the crevices of the wide hardwood planks.

Hugo spread out his arms and kicked lightly, looking down at Mitchell. He exhaled an upward-arching stream of bubbles. If male insects could make babies, he wondered, why couldn't he?


Hugo had met Mitchell on a panel titled, "Nuts for Nutrition: Why Saturated Fat is Good for You." Mitchell was the moderator, then a graduate student from Georgetown who asked easy questions of the well-known scientists and funneled the unanswerable ones to Hugo, an editor for a basement-operation journal. Mitchell approached him later over a tray of rolled deli meat and pickle shears. "You throw me curve balls in front of the audience," Hugo said, "and then flirt with me during the reception."

Mitchell fumbled with his paper plate, a black olive rolling off the edge. "I hope you don't think I was sabotaging you," he stammered. "I mean, it doesn't matter who you are. It's what you bring to the table."

Hugo listened patiently, watching Mitch's biceps tighten in his short-sleeved dress shirt. Mitchell lived in D.C. and was in town to volunteer for the conference. When the reception dwindled he invited Hugo for a drink at the hotel bar. Three vodka martinis led to a nightcap in Mitchell's hotel room, sloppy kisses on the cold balcony overlooking Boston Harbor, and sex with the television tuned to scrolling hotel announcements. For half a year he and Mitchell emailed every day, and once a month picked the other up at the Delta Shuttle gate. On a whim Hugo sent Mitchell a script he'd written for phone sex. They gave up after the first ridiculous attempt, Hugo losing it at Mitchell's dry intonation of the words "love meat."

Hugo's nine-year-old niece Evelina visited for Christmas, coinciding with one of Mitchell's stays. When Mitch suggested they bring her to the Museum of Science Hugo said, "Why not the orthodontist? She could drop in for a quick root canal."

They brought her instead to a touring production of *Hairspray*, explaining as they waited in line before the performance that the show was their Christmas gift to her. "You're kidding, right?" she replied gravely. It had been a running joke ever since.

Mitchell moved into Hugo's floor-through apartment, and during the first year their domestic life was like a Van Gogh painting, the madness barely hidden beneath the bright slathered-on colors. The intensity of their relationship was apparent not only in Mitchell's omelet dinners or their Sunday afternoons at the Museum of Fine Arts, but in their arguments—in the beginning, over small things, unpaid bills, messy closets, sleeping routines. Before long their fights crept into the tenuous territory where insecurity and other men waited.

At work, Hugo began tracking the project of a famous archaeologist in Cairo who was studying the movements of the sun. Each day he measured the length of a ray as it crept across a long cathedral floor, posting his observations on the Web. Hugo bookmarked the site, checking its daily progress. It was just like love: some days the sun blazed with an uncategorical brightness, and other times it crept predictably along its parallax on the marble floor.

When Mitchell began an affair with one of his clients—an Indian architect who ate too many carbs and not enough protein—Hugo felt his anger was half-assed, as if he were upset only because that was how a wronged spouse was supposed to act.

But he wasn't a spouse, was he? Mitchell argued, more like a spousal-equivalent; and though they had been dating then for more than three years, Hugo was neither his husband nor his wife. He was, for lack of a more layered word, his lover. Hugo didn't want to listen to logic. He wanted Mitchell to either end the affair or move out.

Aryana, Hugo's twice-divorced sister, shared her advice for reigning in a husband: babies. "It's all about guilt. There's nothing like a kid to keep them at home." He and Mitchell decided to buy a condo instead.

They moved into an eight-unit brownstone with steep front steps that led to the second floor. The matter of Mitch's affair they packed into their cardboard boxes and moved with them. Hugo agreed to an open relationship. Gay men could do that, Aryana said, avoiding her brother's gaze, just sleep around. And as far as Hugo knew, Mitch was sleeping with half of his clients while he tried to lure Joe the Intern out for a beer. This was the same freckled intern who'd said about him and Mitchell, "You two would have the most beautiful children." He had no idea how prescient he really was.

Hugo woke from his aquatic dream feeling nauseated. He rushed to the bathroom, crouched in front of the toilet, and vomited with his eyes shut. Holding the cold wreath of the seat, he remembered the vinegar-tasting salsa Mitch used to make omelets the previous evening.

He leaned against the porcelain tub and severed the string of saliva from his mouth. Maybe it wasn't the salsa; maybe it was a fever.

"You all right?" Mitch said, staring down at him from the doorway. His gray hair was wild with bed-head. He wore bikini briefs and a black T-shirt.

"Fine. Those eggs," Hugo said.

"Want some water?"

Hugo leaned forward, crossing his arms on his knees. He wanted to be alone.

"I'm fine, Mitch. Go back to bed." Hugo held the edge of the tub and stood.

Mitch scuffed down the hall to their bedroom. Hugo flushed the toilet. He leaned over their wide scallop of a sink, staring at his complexion in the mirror. His skin was ashy, his eyes gaunt. Was it flu season? The term was ridiculous, like all the metaphorical seasons: allergy season, mating season, even Mitch's favorite, tax season. When did they officially begin? And why weren't they sent flyers in advance?

He pulled down his right cheek and stared at the face which long ago had stopped changing—its perfect moon shape, the eyebrows aching to become one, the translucent hairs that covered his cheeks like a kiwi. A big red pimple had made a guest appearance on the tip of his nose. He pinched it between his fingers, suddenly remembering his desire for a baby. Maybe he had morning sickness. He smiled, touching his pudgy stomach and imagining a pea-sized embryo inside. His mother used to talk obsessively about childbirth. She'd had ten children, Hugo the last. *Morning sickness was the easiest part of pregnancy*, she said once. *That queasy feeling eventually passed.*

Dr. Pam, a sixtyish woman who wore little makeup and ponytailed her matronly hair at the nape, had given Hugo small pox vaccinations, prescribed acne medicine and Paxil, and more recently, counseled him on STDs and oral sex. She had been his mother's oldest friend, and argued with her doctors when the cancer spread to his mother's lungs, sharing bedside shifts with Hugo and his nine siblings during the long respirator nights at the end. It was Dr. Pam whom Hugo consulted when his fever and vomiting continued and he woke from fourteen hours of sleep unable to lift himself from bed.

Dr. Pam spent several examinations and three sleepless nights confirming Hugo's pregnancy. In her office she turned on a lightbox on the wall and showed him x-rays. "Scientifically, it's impossible, Hugo, but here, below your bladder, is clearly a womb. This round shape is the head of a developing fetus. And your blood tests repeatedly detect the presence of BhCG, a hormone found exclusively in pregnant women." Hugo listened to Dr. Pam's tempered words, finding the florescent x-rays both fascinating and repulsive. It was his inner organs and a fetus on display. His inner organs! And a fetus! On display!

Dr. Pam wrapped her arm around his shoulders. "Congratulations, Hugo, you are a human platypus."

Hugo slumped in his chair. Dr. Pam smiled, offering to speak for him at a press conference. "But if you want to keep this thing under wraps, it's your decision." She clasped his hand, giving him a mock-stern look. "Miracles aside, the admiration and respect of the medical community mean nothing to me. Really, Hugo, nada."

At his wastepaper basket of a desk—tucked into a corner of the busy *Globe* newsroom—Hugo logged into a chat room and discovered his frequent nosebleeds and constipation were shared by an expectant mother in Brazil. And when Mitchell wanted to have sex, Hugo caved in his chest to keep him from chafing his sensitive nipples. His family and co-editors commented on his weight gain, but as the woolly winds of October descended and he entered his second trimester, Hugo's change to oversized sweaters and snowpants seemed ordinary.

Mitchell urged Hugo to workout. "Just do some cardio, Hugo. Twenty minutes on the bikes," he said one night, as they watched Conan O'Brien banter with his fat sidekick whose name Hugo could never remember. Maybe the fat sidekick was expecting, too. How many men got pregnant each year without anyone finding out?

"You don't have to lift to go to the gym," Mitchell said, kissing Hugo on the cheek before powering off the TV and turning away from him in bed. A minute passed and Hugo thought of a comeback, but Mitchell was already asleep.

Hugo realized, of course, that at some point his massive belly would no longer be concealable. During his ultrasound a short, affable young man with dyed-blue hair (Hugo dubbed him Hefty Smurf) squeezed oily jelly on his stomach, undaunted by the fact of Hugo's pregnancy. Hefty Smurf chatted and pointed out on the monitor the fetus's doll-sized head, its salamander back, the stubs of its webby fingers. "Looks more like a weather map, doesn't it?" he said, handing Hugo a bleary photograph of the fetus. He turned off the scanning tool and wished Hugo good luck.

Hugo latched onto the happy melody of "Girlfriend in a Coma" as he left the examination room and traveled down the quiet corridors of the hospital. That was what was great about The Smiths, the way they got the combination of horror and comedy just right. He entered Dr. Pam's office, humming the bouncy tune. "You're in a devilish mood," she said.

"Pregnancy does that to a man."

He lowered himself into the corduroy chair. What was happening to him? It was as if Mother Nature had loaded up the cargo and set Hugo on a nine-month road trip. Somehow he felt less like a designated driver than a chauffeur.

Dr. Pam ran the green eraser of her pencil down a sheet in Hugo's thick medical folder. "You know, expectant mothers are prone to mood swings. Expectant people, I should say." Dr. Pam closed the file, her voice suddenly deepening into Serious Doctor Mode. "Let's talk game plan, Hugo. You still going to work?"

"I'm thinking of moving to the Isle of Man," he said.

He looked at Dr. Pam, who frowned at him like a wilting flower. She walked around her desk and sat in the matching corduroy chair on his left.

Hugo leaned back and crossed his legs in a figure four. It had become difficult to cross them in his usual way, feminine-like, one knee on top of the other. "I have to make money—I haven't told Mitch yet. He thinks I'm certifiable as it is."

She moved to the window, removing her scrunchie and adjusting her long white hair. "But don't you think it would be easier? I mean, if Mitch loves you—"

Hugo held the ultrasound photo by its corners, turning it clockwise until the hurricane pattern formed a baby. *Did* Mitchell love him? He may have been sleeping around, but Hugo considered sex a physical thing, like this pregnancy. A glint of sun from the snow outside the window made Hugo squint. Maybe love was less like the changing light in Cairo and more like his medical file, a logbook of aches and bruises that had been properly diagnosed. Hugo often thought he and Mitch were as different as butch and lipstick lesbians, but on this Mitch disagreed: he thought they complimented one another. Hugo had once opened a fortune cookie that said, "Wisdom comes from looking backward but life must be lived forward." When Mitch balked at the ersatz proverb, Hugo crumpled the tiny slip of paper and ate it.

Hugo thanked Dr. Pam for her concern and patted her arm, advising her to work on her doctor-patient formality. He creased the ultrasound photo in half, the glossy paper making a squeaking sound. He couldn't say it to Dr. Pam, but in his body, in the space not flooded with amniotic fluid and his small, acrobatic fetus, he believed Mitch loved him.

"I'm pregnant," Hugo said to Mitch at three in the morning. They were seated at the kitchen table, unable to sleep. Insomnia felt as ordinary as walking shoes to Hugo; Mitch, on the other hand, was suffering jet lag from a red-eye trip to San Francisco.

Mitch drank tea and skimmed the Business section of the . *"You're kidding, right?" he said flatly.*

Hugo stood and walked to Mitch. "Feel." He placed Mitch's hand on his large belly. Mitch put down his newspaper and waited. He suddenly felt a faint movement, the murmur of life under his palm.

He yanked his hand away. "Jesus, Hugo! What the hell?"

"It happened the morning I threw up."

"But how—" Mitch said, one brow raised. "It's impossible." He combed his fingers through his graying cowlick. "There's no way."

"Dr. Pam confirmed it. I'm seven months."

Hugo went to the deep metal sink and poured Mitch a glass of water. He set it on their oblong table, sliding it toward his boyfriend. Then he sat in the chair opposite Mitch, their hairy knees touching. Mitch was speechless.

Hugo was convinced the baby had a scent. It was like opening his own Starbucks: repellent to some, attracting a great many others. Joe the Intern was among those who were buying. As they put the science section to bed one Tuesday, Joe asked him if he wanted to grab a beer. Hugo had suffered two nosebleeds that day and a persistent weariness, and though his body told him to go home and rest, the thought of an empty house—Mitchell was out with friends—depressed him.

At a neon-lit sports bar, Hugo sat on a metal bar stool. Joe asked the military-looking bartender for a Rolling Rock, was carded, and refused. With a conciliatory smile, he set a wooden bowl of peanuts in front of Joe and brought Hugo a beer (Dr. Pam had been politesse in her advice to him on alcohol). A gaudy drunk woman at the end of the bar gesticulated to her friend, spilling a martini. Hugo remembered the only time he'd drank a martini, in a dingy hotel bar when he'd met Mitch.

Joe grabbed a handful of nuts and watched the Bruins play on TV. They were like a pair of Before and After posters: Joe the bright-eyed student, Mitch the cynical pseudo-spouse. Why was he here with his intern, watching a hockey game in an empty bar? Was it the possibility of sex? Someone in his chatroom of pregnant women had posted a message that said in the last trimester, the sex had been the best she'd ever had.

Joe turned to him. "You don't look so good, Hugo."

"I'm catching a cold."

"You've been sick a lot lately."

Hugo nodded. He drank the warm beer, hiccupping after a few sips.

Joey cleared his throat. "You live with someone, right?"

"My partner."

The freckled boy glanced at the television above Hugo's head. "The older guy? In that picture on your bulletin board?"

"His name is Mitch," Hugo said.

"So you're *gay*?" Joe whispered "gay" as if uttering the word would immediately transform him into Nathan Lane.

Hugo realized the direction of Joe's conversation. In his womb the baby did cartwheels, scratching its partially formed spine against Hugo's back. He repositioned himself on the stool. "Yes, Joe, I am gay," he said, reluctantly playing therapist. Hugo liked his self-image of the smart young editor too hip for labels.

"Like, when did you know?" Joe asked. The boy squared himself on the stool and faced Hugo, his elbow resting on the bar.

Hugo finished his beer and asked the bartender for a glass of water. Joe ordered a Sprite. Ten years out, he tried to remember the boy's fear, that desperate feeling that hinged on whether you came out or married some hapless girl, fathered children, cruised public rest rooms like Larry Craig for the rest of your life. For nearly an hour Hugo shared the details of his life with Joe—the way he threw up before he came out to his mother, meeting Mitch at the conference, being out at work—and when the bartender brought them their tab, Hugo paid the bill. Then Hugo lied, asking Joe to excuse him. Mitch was cooking omelets for them at home.

"The trend now is toward drugs," said Dr. Pam, her fingers intertwined on the glass desk. "Lamaze went the way of vinyl. Nowadays, Mom wants labor to be as easy as getting a facial."

Mitch had finally agreed to meet with Dr. Pam. They were seated in her office, separated from her by the glass desk, a sleek laptop computer, and a chrome penholder that looked like two lobster antennae. Hugo pressed his leg against Mitch's in the seat next to him. His get-up today was a loose, knee-length parka and sweatpants. Mitch was wearing chinos and a dress shirt; he had come straight from a diet consultation with a client.

Mitchell tapped his foot in measured beats on the carpet.

Dr. Pam sensed his impatience. "What's on your mind, Mitch?"

He rolled his eyes. "I'm wondering why you're entertaining Hugo's delusions."

Mitch lifted his blazer from the back of his chair and slipped into it. "Forget it. I'm going home." He stood and went to the door. When he reached for the L-shaped handle, he stopped and turned to Hugo. His face was impatient, searching.

"Are you coming?"

Hugo looked at Dr. Pam. What he wanted was to stay where he was. He longed to say to Mitch, "Sit down, listen to what Dr. Pam has to say." What he wanted, more than anything, was for Mitch to act like an expectant father, or mother. If pressed, he would have asked for a little peace and maybe some Louis Armstrong-wonder at the world. Instead, Hugo lifted himself from the chair and took Mitch's open hand, uttering an apologetic farewell to Dr. Pam as she called his name from behind her glass desk.

In Hugo's daydream he was naked and also a jumbo jet. The sky was pure blue, the earth below him the crumbly texture of a cookie. He drifted slowly, idling, sailing through thin skeets of clouds. In his belly—the plane's cabin—his tropical-storm fetus pawed the walls of his stomach with its webby hands. There was something both exciting and irritating about its presence; Hugo put one arm-wing to his middle and picked at the tightened skin, as if it were a price tag he could remove without leaving any sticky residue.

"What if it's not mine?" Mitch asked that night in bed.

"What are you talking about? Of course it's yours."

"You've been sleeping around, right?"

Mitchell held the remote control, idly changing channels. Hugo was making a list of baby names: Grover, Monroe, Obama. For some reason they kept coming out presidential. What kind of response would Milhaus receive on the jungle gym?

"How can I convince you?" Hugo asked.

"I'm throwing out questions. You always think I'm trying to sabotage you."

"It's yours, Mitch. There isn't anybody else."

"But I thought we agreed—"

"We agreed to be open. That doesn't mean I went out and screwed the first jarhead I saw."

"You mean, you haven't—?"

"With who? And when do you think I had time, between sneaking to doctor's appointments and working late on the paper?"

"But don't you want to?"

Hugo tucked his ballpoint pen behind his ear. He didn't care as much as Mitchell did about sex. Hugo placed his list of names on the milk crates. "I guess the opportunity never came up."

Mitchell turned off the TV and was silent. He rolled away from Hugo and faced the painted wall.

Hugo felt the baby kicking, the surprising jerks like desperate kernels of popcorn. He said, "It's okay, Milhaus," and rolled flat on his back, pulling the blanket to his chin.

Mitch turned and faced him. "Definitely not Milhaus," Mitch said, placing his hand gently on Hugo's stomach. "Christ. I thought only straight guys had to worry about getting their girlfriends pregnant."

Hugo chose a natural childbirth. The thought of pain was terrifying, but if he was going to be the first man ever to give birth, he felt a responsibility to be the first man to actually give birth, not cheat the process with an epidermal like some freakish animal on a bed-table. He hired a portly midwife named Rosie with a mane of Aqua Net to teach him to breathe on his and Mitch's braided living room rug.

Now, in a breezy room overlooking the entrance of Brigham and Women's Hospital, Hugo breathed calmly. His contractions were spaced nearly ten minutes apart.

He squeezed Rose's callused hand, sucking in his cheeks and saying, "This is the part of the movie where the woman starts bitching out the man."

Mitch held Hugo's other hand. He stood above Hugo, who lay on his back with knees bent on the soft opium bed.

"And the man agrees with everything," Mitch said, "because he knows that he is solely responsible for the baby, man's suffering, and yes, all evil in the world."

Hugo smiled, the pain receding for a moment.

Dr. Pam entered and placed a hand on Mitch's shoulder. To Hugo she said, "It looks like you're doing just fine." She looked to where Rose, her friend, had pulled up a stool at the foot of the bed. "How many kids have you birthed now, Rose? It's gotta be up to fifty."

"Fifty-two. Mrs. Kaburagi gave birth to twins yesterday." Rose handed Mitch a wet towel and he dabbed it on Hugo's forehead in small swiveling gestures. "But this baby is special, I know it."

Hugo thought: special, and premature. The contractions began to quicken and Hugo could feel nothing outside his pain and the coin-sized hole in his body that this baby was struggling to get its head through. He labored in a dense fog of immediacy. For one fleeting moment he imagined his mother prostrate in this same position, the pain she had endured to give birth to him and his siblings.

Tears ran down Hugo's cheeks when the baby was born—out of joy or relief, he didn't know—and later, after she died and was placed soundlessly in his arms. They were the first moments in Hugo's life that had felt real, cradling his lifeless daughter, combing her fine wet hair with his palm. Was this the experience men were never supposed to understand?

The bright April morning Hugo was released, Mitchell pushed him in a shiny wheelchair down a hospital corridor. Something about the length of the hallway reminded him of the cathedral in Cairo, its tile path for the sun embedded in the marble floor. Hugo passed an operating room with surgeons huddled in green scrubs, a waiting area with more toddlers than adults, a row of brown doors (all closed), and more operating rooms and more waiting areas. On the first floor, Mitchell pushed Hugo through the electric doors to the cracked sidewalk.

He looked up at Mitch, his house keys jangling at his waist. Aryana had asked him once what he saw in Mitchell; he'd answered something sentimental that he couldn't remember now. Mitch kissed Hugo quickly on the cheek and told him to wait while he retrieved the car.

Leaves shimmered on the maple trees around the edge of the parking lot like great green waves. A VW bug and a bulky ambulance were idling beneath the canopy, and the people entering or leaving the hospital were bunched in groups and pairs.

Hugo wanted to revise his answer to Aryana about Mitch. I see silver-blue eyes and graying hair, he thought, pushing himself up in the wheelchair, I see sunlight fading on a cathedral floor.

*Ricco Siasoco is a Boston-based writer and professor born and raised in Iowa. His fiction has been published in* the North American Review, Flyway Literary Review, Drunken Boat, Memorious, *and* the Boston Phoenix*, among others, and anthologized in* Take Out: Queer Writing from Asian Pacific America *(Asian Am. Writers' Workshop, 2001),* Screaming Monkeys *(Coffee House Press, 2003)* and Walang Hiya: Literature Taking Risks Toward Liberatory Practice *(Carayan Press, 2010). He has received fellowships from the Fine Arts Work Center in Provincetown, the LEF Foundation, and PEN New England, and holds an MFA from the Bennington Writing Seminars. He currently teaches creative writing at Boston College.*

Los Angeles

# A CRAIGSLIST AD FOR A MINDBLOWING
# SELF-ACTUALIZATION PARTY
## Margaret Wappler

A half-Japanese man and an artistic woman seek companionship for an all-night party in which we will rip open our souls and spear out the tangy ego with a cocktail fork. We live off of Mulholland Drive in a painfully minimalist pad with the kind of turquoise swimming pool that's witnessed a few instances of virgin blood and a couple of near-fatal overdoses. But let that darkness motivate you to form a tender militia outfitted in gauze and amethyst, linen and leather, who will march from Cold Canyon Road into our home that we've rented from a fallen '90s director with an autistic son. If you can see auras or feel vibrations— and we prefer those who can— you can glide your hand over the sleek smoked glass of our home and feel the snapped-off dreams of all its residents, past and present. In the living room, where we once grappled on the floor after a rough night of too much cocaine and a confessed abortion, the aura is a pulsating, sweaty purple that starts screaming like a schizophrenic little girl obsessed with cats and numbers if you're on enough mushrooms. If you're really deep, you can set your hands upon the stone-tile floor and feel the constant tremor, the lowdown talky rumble of the Big One, coming any day now to eat us, eat us, eat us all. This seismic clusterfuck, once it dawns, will open The Great Chasm of California, a goddess of monstrous demand with an open shuddering mouth, into which all the people of Los Angeles will fall, delicate figurines exploding at the bottom, spraying out champagne and implant juice, bottled water and matcha tea, exhuming smog and rare medicinal marijuana strains from their lungs and pores. But before any of that happens— and this is our only hope for staving off the faultline's rupture for a little while longer— we must tap into the great divine, the spirit rapture, the buzzing grid of the self united with other selves to make one knotty dreadlock of self-actualization. Let's tip into awe together. Let's make friends we can also fuck. Let's find a giant vat of gold-speckled oil and anoint each other in a frenzy of writhing limbs and torsos, set to the music of a band whose biggest claim to fame is playing every Monday at the Waikiki Hilton but somebody's invested a ridiculous amount of money in them so the CD has been forced upon the hosts of this party. Children, plants, pets and skeptics welcome. We have compassion for all: Namo Kuan Shi Yin Pusa. Namo Kuan Shi Yin Pusa. Namo Kuan Shi Yin Pusa. Namo Kuan Shi Yin Pusa. See you soon...

It is OK to repost this ad.

*Margaret Wappler's work has been published in* the Los Angeles Times, The Believer, Rolling Stone, Fader, Arthur Magazine, Another Chicago Magazine *and* Black Clock. *She is a graduate of the MFA Program in Critical Studies at California Institute of the Arts.*

Toronto

## SISSY
Zoe Whittall

### 1.

Sauntering down Aisle 6 at the 24-hour Dominion grocery store, Lee is cradling an overly large zucchini. It sits inside the sleeve of his thick pea-green parka, where he is pretending to house a broken limb. He conjures the cast's hard shell and the way he'd have to lay on the couch watching daytime TV instead of dishwashing for eight hours at a time. He considers breaking his elbow, a swift snap. Then it wouldn't be a lie.

Lee has a strange relationship to the truth. The truth sticks her tongue in his mouth obsessively. She runs her hand up his leg, almost, whispering, *Why are you shoplifting a zucchini, you fucking idiot?* Lee suspects he has latent Tourette's, what with these voices coming in sharp spurts, accompanied by a shudder or a shoulder tick.

Lately the truth is too much. Last week, there was a staff party at the restaurant. Everyone got too drunk. His girlfriend Linda was throwing up in the bathroom downstairs in the basement for what seemed like hours. Kevin, the other dishwasher and Lee's sometimes after-work friend, disappeared. When Lee finally found Linda, she'd been hit in the face, her dress torn. She couldn't tell him what had happened until the next day, and it was all in pieces. She kept saying, *It was Kevin, but it was more like a Kevin imposter. He was a monster. I kept pushing him off me, but he wouldn't stop.*

Lee brushes away the truth's impalpable hand, walks toward the front cash.

"The worst thing is the itching," he tells the cashier, a bottle redhead, who nods sympathetically as he pays for a pack of cinnamon gum.

"I broke my wrist last year. It sucked," she says. Lee feels a slippery worm of guilt sliding down the back of his throat. The woman shifts from anonymous cashier to someone with bones that can fracture and heal. He slides the gum in the back pocket of his fading black work pants.

Sometimes Lee uses a crutch. Once, a fake wheelchair stolen by his older brother Dan to use for scams.

Tucked in his Y-front briefs is steak wrapped in Styrofoam. In his right boot is powdered gravy. Up his other sleeve a slim candy bar, for good luck. Always take something from right up front if you're going to bother.

Lee comes from criminals. "It's in your blood," Dan told him as a kid. "Forget working class, we're thieving class." He'd pump up his chest, throwing Lee over his shoulder like a sack of potatoes while Lee kicked and giggled, yelling, *Let me down! Put me down! Stop!* Before Dan finally laid him out on the grass of their yard and tickled him until he yelled *Mercy!*

Lee still shoplifts on occasion, but he doesn't do anything else illegal. He has vowed to stop stealing as soon as he makes an annual income above the poverty line. He has never hit anyone or stolen money from a person. He is an anomaly in his family, and he likes it that way.

Lee is thin and lanky, almost girly. Blondish hair, shy smile. His voice lilts a little, higher than most men, and he is often called a fag because of this. Miraculously, despite his femininity, he has never been beaten up or fought anyone. As a kid, Dan was always around to fight for him, and as an adult, he managed to avoid it. He never wanted to hit anyone before. It was what separated him from the rest of his family—the fact that he could avoid it. He counts himself lucky and always had. His adult life was filled with things he created so carefully: good friends, warm holidays, minimal conflict.

Six days ago, it was as though all of his warmth, all of his luck he lived with, was thrown into an industrial blender. He looked at his limbs and couldn't tell if they were his. Is this my arm? Drop a dish. You'd be surprised how good it feels. To watch shards of white restaurant plates finish their purposeful lives and get swept away into giant dustbins caked with blackened grease and dirt.

*What the fuck is your problem?* Eyebrow twitch. He shakes his shoulders around to calm his muscular outbursts.

Lee is trying to look forward to supper. George and Stephanie invited him over to get away, out of the house. Steph will bake something weird like a buttermilk pie. She's very *Little House on the Prairie* right now. She's declared a household embargo against beer and pizza, and has taken to doing things like making her own crackers and dehydrating her own fruit. She always makes cordial and serves it in tall parfait glasses with silly straws. Exotic fruit cut up in the shape of stars and hearts on the side of the plate. She likes presentation. She has a lot of fruit scrubs and a lotion that smells like cookies in her tiny bathroom.

George and Stephanie are one of those couples who would shake the foundation of all your beliefs if they ever broke up; a ball of yarn in complementary colors. They have weekly dinner parties with Lee and other friends, but this is the first one since the staff party. They wanted Linda to come, for her to feel comforted and distracted, but she declined the invitation.

The snow crunches underneath Lee's work boots. Sounds like the crack in his jaw where he holds all of his tension. He walks up Brunswick Avenue a little shoplifting-high, a little remorseful. Mostly hungry and blank. He can't help wondering when his brain will return, as if it was erased by what happened.

Lee has stopped plotting to hurt Kevin for the first time in six days. Squeeze, or kick, or punch him until he cries. He is trying to make peace with the situation, going against his mother's suggestion to "kick the living shit outta that waste of skin," at Linda's pleading to "just let it go."

All other days have gone as follows:

Bring Linda breakfast in bed, wait until it is congealed and she is still staring up at the ceiling. Take it away. Stand in living room with daytime television on for noise. *"My Teen Daughter Wants to Be a Stripper and a Humanitarian!"* Bring her bouquets of flowers, novelty candy from the store across from Future Bakery, books of poetry from Book City. Remind her to go to counseling appointment, doctor. Shuffle in her mother, her sister, Steph, who is her best friend. Apply arnica to her bruises. Hold her if she cries. She only cries once, usually, before Lee goes to work.

Linda talks. There was a guy in high school, her swim coach. There was a trial, a jail sentence, a school divided. Linda is reminded of it all, and can't go outside. When the coach went to jail, six months plus probation, she didn't feel satisfied. Still, people avoided her.

Blamed her. When Lee suggested calling the cops about Kevin, Linda said, *Why bother? Didn't work the first time.*

Outside is too much. Lee is trying to be a good boyfriend, support her, but he is completely uncertain what to do.

He goes to work at the restaurant and works an eight-hour shift dishwashing. Lee calls her on the hour.

"I'm fine, don't worry so much. I'm just, tired."

"Do you need anything?"

"I need you to not do anything stupid. Bye."


When she hangs up, always first, Lee rests his head against the brown grease-stained wall next to the pinned-up schedule and tries to breathe. Lee's name is written in red marker eleven days in a row. He has no days off because Kevin quit so suddenly, just didn't show up the day after the staff party.

Kevin. Lee can't even think his name without his eyes going out of focus, the dirty floor paneling shifting. Kevin. Lee blacks out all the Kevins that appear on the January work calendar. Out of ink. Tries again with his nail. His nails have grown long from neglect.

He brings the mop water out into the alley to dump and looks up to the third story window where Kevin lives above the restaurant. He thinks it would be too easy, to walk up the stairs, break down the door. Instead, Lee goes back into the kitchen, where every move his body makes feels leaden and irritating. When he thinks there may be a lull long enough for a smoke break, another table clears, another grease-caked pan arrives.

After punching out, he declines invitations to go next door for pints and pinball and instead climbs up the fire escape of Kevin's building.

He watches through the window. Kevin's in red jogging pants and a shirt that says "I Survived the Black-Out 03." He smokes and flicks the remote. Picks at the knee hole in his pants. His girlfriend sleeps on the armchair. It's the same every night. Stops to roll joints on a TV guide. Eventually falls asleep. Lee looks for signs of distress in his face, guilty dark bags under his eyes. Finds nothing.

Lee goes home when a woman startles him, walking through the alley muttering to herself. He notices his fingers are numb, and he's lost his nerve. If there was one thing valuable he learned from his brother it's that you don't want to go to jail. The voices of reason beat the voices that chastise and degrade.


## 2.


Stephanie is doing pretty well, considering Linda is her best friend. George is one of those people who deals with tragedy very calmly. He has been writing letters to the community paper about safety for women in the neighborhood. He has been examining his life and begun using phrases like "I've been noticing my male privilege."

George has never seen a crime that he wasn't watching on television. He thought it would feel different, that it would feel monumental. His own composure scares him.

Stephanie is all *life goes on,* and *it coulda been worse,* and *she'll heal and move on.* Steph had a gun in her mouth during a hold up at the Cash Mart, a father who locked her in a closet for three days, and scar in her left foot where someone once stabbed her when she bartended at a strip club.


When Lee arrives for dinner at the apartment that Stephanie and George share with some other kids from school, she notices his TV-dinner eyes. His complexion is an old dishrag.

"You look good," she says, giving him a friendly hug. Stephanie regards her position amongst their peer group as Den Mother, emotional glue stick, party starter, and conflict mediator.

Stephanie watches silently while Lee reaches into his pants, pulls out the steak. She grabs his red offering and smiles warmly, careful to hold his gaze, hoping to transmit some comfort. She's worried for him. He doesn't seem right. Even though she knew he was sensitive, erratic, a soft little boy with the exterior of a lanky slacker comic book artist.

She sits Lee down on the couch and runs her hands over his head before going into the kitchen to bring out a tray of lime cordials. George is finishing up a PlayStation game while Stephanie tells Lee about her latest art project embroidering internal organs on the outside of cowboy shirts.

Lee seems pretty calm, considering, being around his friends.

"So, Linda doesn't want to come eh?"

"No."

"I made buttermilk pie—her favorite."

"Yeah," Lee says, shrugging. "She's still taking those sleeping pills the doctor gave her."

The dinner table is set with a frilly lace tablecloth and fancy china Stephanie bought at an antique sale two weeks ago. A plastic pitcher with Strawberry Shortcake is filled with strawberry daiquiri. "My latest eBay conquest," Stephanie says, filling the metallic pink pint glasses with the pulpy liquid.

All three take bites and chew methodically. When they are done, George clears the dishes away and Stephanie prepares the pie and ice cream.

Lee says it first.

"I want to hurt him."

Stephanie says, fork clinking on china, "I want to kill him."

George raises his eyebrows a bit. Closes his eyes tightly, turns red. "We could probably get away with it."

Anna, their cherubic roommate walks into the kitchen, mumbles, "Hey." She looks like a commercial for facial cleanser. She goes into the living room and turns on the television. The sound of *The Simpsons* fills the apartment. The one where Maggie shoots Mr. Burns.

"I love this one," they say simultaneously, getting up and heading toward the other room.

### 3.

Lee goes to the bathroom and throws up. George watches TV with Anna. Stephanie chain-smokes. Lee watches the swirls of former pie turn and he thinks he might faint. He rests his head on the toilet bowl, snivels, squeezes his eyes shut.

*What am I supposed to do with this? How can I live with this?*

The truth climbs up his spine, says, *You're just going to have to.*

Lee knows that he is the worst person to ever live. He hadn't fully believed it before. He protested vehemently his own self-worth. But here it was, staring him in the face while the creamy vomit swirled down. Like his mom used to say, "You're fucking *nothing.* You sissy little shit, you'll never be anything."

The memory of his mother's voice sometimes sounds like the truth, the same soft woman, insistent and composed. It confuses him. He heaves again.

Leaving the washroom, George hands the cordless to Lee with an anxious look on this face. Linda says, "I hear something outside. I can't breathe."

Lee grabs his coat and runs out to the street, keeps a steady pace the whole two blocks home. He climbs into bed with her, still wearing his parka and sloppy snow-covered work boots. She is staring at the ceiling. He holds her and falls asleep there, dreams about eating fish sticks made from dead prime ministers. When he tells Linda about the dream, it's the first time he's heard her laugh since it happened.

The next day Lee comes out of the kitchen at work, wipes his wet, pruned hands on his apron, and walks to the bar to have a smoke. George is sitting there nursing a pint, "Hey, I was waiting for you to take a break. Come with me." He takes Lee by the arm, weaves through the tables, and out into the street, even though they are both wearing T-shirts and the snow melts on their pale arms. He stops three doors down at a storefront window. Looking in they can see a self-defense class in session.

"I've been watching them for an hour," George says. "And I think I know how to do it, how we could really fuck Kevin up, you know, make him pay for what he did."

"Are we going to kick him in the groin until he dies?" Lee asks, laughing. Inside, a sweaty blond in a ponytail is kicking a padded person that looks like the marshmallow man from *Ghostbusters*.

"Well," says George, who is even more girly than Lee, more timid and non-confrontational, has never so much as landed a punch, Lee guesses.

"We need Stephanie," Lee says.

They run around the corner to George and Steph's apartment. Stephanie is doing crunches on the living room floor, listening to Michael Jackson's *Off The Wall*.

"How are we going to do it?" George says, panting.

"Why aren't you guys wearing coats? Do what?"

"Kill Kevin."

She sits up, takes the small pink towel from around her neck and dabs at her forehead.

"What the fuck are you talking about? I just said I wanted him dead. I didn't say I was going to kill him."

The boys sit down and light smokes. Rub their numbing arms with couch pillows.

"Isn't your break over?" George asks.

Lee is startled. "Holy shit, I forgot I was still working!"

Lee runs out the door and crosses the street moving fast into the parking lot, ducks into the back door of the restaurant. A backload of dishes, resentful looks from the waiter who hates him. He feels energized, like maybe something will happen, maybe they can make Kevin feel some sort of forced empathy for what he did. They don't have to kill him, just fuck him up a bit. Like a beat down. Like in rap videos.

Kevin is waiting outside in the alley when Lee goes out to dump out the mop water after closing. His face is a blank glazed donut. Lee feels cheated, that this wasn't what he planned.

They stare, a foot apart, like two cowboys in a standoff. Kevin starts to speak,    "Look, Lee, I don't really remember everything, I was so wasted, man."

The crowd in the bar next door cheers after the Leafs score a goal.

Lee's heart is the only thing he hears. His mouth is dry. He lifts the mop out of the bucket, slopping water all over the pavement. He pushes Kevin up against the brick wall, pins his chest with the mop handle.

"You don't *remember? That's* your excuse?"

Instinct takes over. It must be in his blood, this violence.


*Zoe Whittall is the author of the Lambda Award-winning novel* Holding Still for as Long as Possible. *A critically acclaimed fiction writer and poet, her debut,* Bottle Rocket Hearts, *was* a Globe and Mail *"Top 100" pick and a* Quill & Quire *Best Book.*

New York

## SKIN
## Kevin Wilson

Tonight, before they cross the street to their neighbors' house, Tommy and Margo wrap their seven-year-old boy, Caleb, in his winter coat and mittens and hat until he is not their son but a bundle of clothes in the shape of a boy. The wind carries the snow across the yard, thin, powdery curls snapping in the air, an angry cold. "It's just a short walk," Margo tells her son, who squirms inside the clothes, embarrassed that this much fuss is being made over him. "And it'll be worth it," his father says, patting the boy's coat to reassure himself that his son is inside. "We're gonna have fun."

The families have started getting together once a week to play cards and watch *Hee-Haw*, to drink beer and unwind. They are the youngest couples in the subdivision on Fawn Drive, each with a child, in houses nearly identical. Though Tommy and Margo have moved here less than six months ago, they can imagine themselves always living in this town, and they are happy to have other people to spend that time with, playing cards, watching *Hee-Haw*. It is a good enough life.

They walk though the snow with a six-pack of Pabst Blue Ribbon and a dip made with guacamole and beans and cheese and black olives covered in aluminum foil. Tommy carries the six pack under one arm and holds Caleb in the other, holstered on his hip. They move through the snow and wind and cold fifty yards to the Kimball house, where they know they will be happy for a few hours at least.

Caleb wraps his arms tightly around his father's neck and watches through the slit of open space between his hat and scarf as they approach the house. He can see activity through the big window in the Kimballs' living room, the parents setting chairs around the card table, a fire already going. Kammi, the Kimballs' daughter who is one year younger than him, is waving to them, inviting them closer and closer. "There's your girlfriend," Tommy says to his son, though the wind obscures his words. "I think she wants a kiss."

Though they mention it only in jest, to tease their children, both couples would be happy if Caleb and Kammi became sweethearts, got married, lived in a house close to them and carried on much the same way they have. It would suit everyone just fine and when they watch their children playing, bobbing up and down on the hobbyhorse and whooping like Indians, they look at each other and smile. They collectively think how nice it would be, how simple and perfect, which most simple things seem to be.

It is Margo especially who would like to see this happen, sooner rather than later. She is weighed down with vague flashes of her son and why he sometimes seems like a foreign object in her house. She has caught Caleb over the past year, crouched in the corner of his room, pants down at his ankles. She will open the door and find him positioned like that in the far corner of the room, touching himself in those places that she would rather not have to think about. Sometimes she closes the door softly and walks back into the living room and reads biographies of American presidents. She is up to Franklin Pierce, who was neither mediocre nor capable, merely a caretaker, which many of these men seemed to be.

Other times however, when the moment seems to fill up her lungs and flush her face, she grabs Caleb and spanks him, his pants already down and therefore convenient. She never tells him why she is doing this, only ever slaps at his legs and rear with a fierce silence. Her son never asks either, what it is that he has done wrong, because he has some vague idea, a notion, or else he wouldn't be in the far corner of his room.

It is what he reads that frightens Margo, his comic books always opened and spread on the floor around him while he sits there in the corner. After she has sent him out to the back yard to pull weeds or swing or just go away for a while, she gathers up the comics, looking at the pictures that makes Caleb do the things he does. He always has the comic book of the Sub Mariner opened, a muscular, pointy-eared man who lives underwater. He wears nothing but green, scaly swimming trunks and on his ankles are a pair of tiny wings, small like the wings of the tooth fairy. It is disconcerting to Margo in ways she cannot explain, obscene. There is something she does not understand about her son and these pictures of men in capes, bursting with muscles. Those tiny wings. Her son is mysterious to her, something she had not expected to happen for many years.

When they get inside, Sammy Kimball takes the beer and his wife, Tammi, takes the dip, while Margo and Tommy get Caleb out of his snow gear. The process is more time-intensive than any of them believe is necessary for a fifty-yard walk across the street.

After he has struggled out of his jacket and snow pants, Caleb sits at the counter with Kammi while the adults talk about the week, their jobs, and sit down for cards. The house is warm and smells of wood smoke and fried bologna. There is a George Jones song on the record player, singing something about not taking your love to town. Margo lays out the dip with some corn chips and Tammi sets out a plate of cold fried chicken and fried bologna sandwiches. Everyone opens a beer and the night seems easily understandable, something that can be held in the palm of their hand.

Once they've eaten their sandwiches, Kammi takes Caleb into her room, the scent of eucalyptus and rosemary, and dumps a bucket of crayons onto the carpet. She shuts the door behind them and Caleb reaches underneath the bed for the flashlights. They crawl into the closet, a walk-in that is filled with Kammi's clothes and stacks of old magazines and newspapers that won't fit anywhere else. They take a handful of crayons and begin to draw on the walls, hidden behind the row of clothes hanging like a curtain.

This is something they have been doing for weeks, a secret they know will be discovered, which somehow makes it even more necessary.

After a few awkward weeks of playing, Kammi quickly losing interest and then yanking him into another game whether he wanted to or not, Caleb had shown Kammi a book his mother had given him, with Indians and these strange, simplistic figures drawn on the walls of caves. Actually the book was about some young brave who loses his favorite bow, but that didn't interest Caleb as much as the drawings. He and Kammi stared at the images, charcoal scribbles of stick figures riding lines that somehow suggested the form of a horse. It seemed like something manageable, a simple form of art. It was made all the more desirable by the fact that these pictures were drawn on walls, forbidden by parents. Kammi then walked into her closet and took a black crayon and drew a person walking over water, the waves of the ocean like a dozen shark fins. Caleb took a color that was called Ochre, which seemed Indian enough, and drew flaming arrows being shot over mountains, the peaks again looking much like the ocean waves Kammi had drawn, a school of sharks.

Now they have filled nearly the entire wall, simple strokes, lines of dark colors, bends and curves suggesting so much movement the wall seems to vibrate. Caleb draws a cloud, heavy with rain, spitting tiny dots of rain onto a group of grazing cows, heads bowed to the earth. Next to him, Kammi quickly scratches a quiver's worth of arrows into the body of a man, cowboy hat atop his head. She then reaches for the red crayon, worn down to a nub, to bring the blood flowing out of his body, pooling at his feet. Kammi's drawings sometimes scare Caleb, Indians falling off cliffs, dogs tearing a sheep apart, things spilling their insides. She holds the red crayon tight between her fingers and digs into the wall, laughing softly with delight.

The children hidden away, the couples switch partners. Margo stares across the table at Sammy, who is smiling at her, shuffling the cards. Tommy returns to the table with a beer for Margo and kisses her on her forehead, which makes Sammy smile even harder. The cards circle around the table, scooped up in hands and quickly arranged. Tommy bids four and Margo bids two; she could perhaps get four but she prefers to play it safe, to slowly accumulate points while the other team jumps up and down. Tammi bids three and now Sammy, looking at his cards and then at Margo, back and forth, until finally he says, "Margo, I'm going nil." Margo frowns. "I can only get two, Sammy. You can't go nil." Sammy places his cards down on the table and points to Margo.

"You gotta be more adventurous, sweetie. Tell her Tommy." Tommy is concentrating on the cards in his left hand and biting into the chicken leg held in his right. "Be more adventurous, sweetie," Tommy says. Margo looks up at Sammy and he winks at her. Margo shivers and, unsure of what else to do, she starts rearranging the cards in her hand.

A month ago, nearly two in the morning, Margo sat on the couch in the living room and read another presidential biography. They had gone out for pizza and then taken Caleb to the comic book store for the newly released books he'd been saving his allowance for. He and Tommy walked around the store, flipping through the comics, while Margo waited in the car. Caleb came back with another Sub-Mariner, a Marvel Team-Up with Spider-Man and Captain America, and something called Ka-Zar, a blonde, nearly naked, muscle-bound caveman of some sorts, riding a saber-tooth tiger on the cover. Tommy pulled the car onto the main drag and said, "The boy loves his comic books, no doubt about that."

Now, still awake in the middle of the night, both of the men in her house fast asleep, Margo went into the kitchen for a glass of milk. She drank it in big gulps, standing over the sink, staring out the window into the darkness outside. Out of the corner of her eye, she saw someone, standing in front of their bedroom window, a man standing on his toes, face pressed against the screen of the window. Before she could think better of it, to yell for her husband, lights going on all over the house, she opened the window and whispered into the night, "Hello?" The figure spun around, something in his hands, and stumbled away from the house. "Yeah?" he said, and Margo realized it was her neighbor. "Sammy?" she asked and there was a brief pause before she heard him reply, "Oh, Margo? That you?" Sammy took off his cap to further prove his identity, to calm her, but Margo still wasn't sure what was happening. "Are you okay, Sammy?" she asked, and she could barely make out the smile break across his face. "Couldn't sleep," he said.

Sammy was now standing in front of the kitchen window, Margo feeling the cold on her bare legs, one of Tommy's T-shirts hanging down to her knees. She saw that Sammy was holding a plastic ring of beer cans, only three left. "Are you drunk, Sammy?" she asked.

He shook his head. "Not even close," he said. "I just couldn't sleep, nothing on TV, and I thought Tommy might want to have a few. He's asleep though, isn't he?" Margo nodded. "Sleeping like a baby," Sammy said, shuffling his feet. He pulled a beer from the plastic and held it up to the window. "You wouldn't want one, would you?" he asked.

"It's late, Sammy," she said. "I'm going back to bed."

Sammy popped the top on the beer and took a heavy sip. "You won't tell Tommy about this, will you?" he asked. Margo laughed, and then frowned at having done so.

"I don't know what I'd tell him," she said. "I don't know what's going on." Sammy smiled and finished the rest of the beer.

"Let's just pretend it was a dream," he said. He crumpled the can in his hand and slipped it into his jacket pocket. "Go back to sleep," he said and walked across the street to his house. Margo slid the window shut, but she couldn't walk away from the sink, gazing at the spot where Sammy had just been. She stayed awake for another hour, waiting for Sammy's face to reappear at the window, and she could not understand, or even acknowledge, the disappointment that she felt when he did not return.

Two go-rounds into the hand, Sammy throws down a king of clubs that Margo can't cover, losing the nil. Margo slaps the table. "Damn it, Sammy," she says, which makes everyone else laugh. Sammy holds his hands up in surrender. "We'll do it your way now," he says. "I'll behave."

Birds are falling out of the sky onto spikes jutting out of the ground, but Caleb tries to stay focused on the project as Kammi scribbles furiously beside him. Underneath the waves of the ocean, he draws a small figure swimming, arms outstretched, bubbles rising from his mouth. Caleb takes the Gunmetal crayon and draws two pairs of wings on the figure's ankles. Kammi notices the picture and draws an octopus near the Sub-Mariner, one tentacle moving closer and closer to Caleb's drawing. "Let's leave him alone," Caleb asks and Kammi stops drawing. She nods her agreement and it makes Caleb smile to have saved his drawing.

They crawl out of the closet, into the light of the room, and lay on their stomachs, sorting through the pile of crayons. The air is heavy with steam from the vaporizer, which the Kimball's keep on every evening during the winter because Kammi is always congested and slow with colds. They watch the machine's steady exhalations of steam, like a dragon crouched in the corner of the room. Caleb and Kammi line up the crayons according to shade, from dark to light, and then they select what they want to take back into the closet.

Before they go back, Kammi puts her crayons down and touches Caleb's face, strokes his cheek. Last week, Kammi pressed her lips against Caleb's and hummed, the thrumming of her voice tickling his teeth. Kammi likes to touch him, running her finger down the back of his neck, pulling off his shoes and socks and counting his toes. Caleb doesn't know how to respond when this happens, stands very still and counts to ten. "I don't want to draw anymore," Kammi says, and Caleb asks her what she wants to do instead. "Let's play house," she offers and he agrees, unsure of what to do next. "You lie down," she says, "and I'll get on top of you." They lie together in silence like this, their breathing not quite in rhythm. "Close your eyes," Kammi says, and Caleb does. He feels her pulling on his shirt, baring his stomach, and then she lies down on him again, the skin of their stomachs touching. After a few seconds of silence, the weight of Kammi pressing into him, he opens his eyes and finds her face less than an inch from his, her eyes wide open. "We're still playing," she says. "Keep your eyes closed."

Tommy and Tammi have won the last two hands and so they switch partners again, the men against the women. As they trade chairs, refilling their plates and opening fresh beers, Tammi asks if anyone wants to smoke some pot. "It's pretty good, Tommy," Sammy says, "This guy, some roofer who hangs out at the bowling alley on Wednesdays, gets it from Florida. And they get it from some island further south." Tommy looks at Margo who doesn't want to say no in front of Sammy and Tammi, but won't allow herself to say yes. Tommy nods in her direction, his eyes asking for her approval. "Maybe a small one," she finally says and Tommy pulls her close to him. "I only know how to roll big ones," Sammy says, "so I guess we'll only smoke half."

The door to the garage open, the four adults pass the joint around, inhaling deeply and then directing the smoke out the door and into the garage, a cloud sitting heavy beside the Kimballs' car. "Let's hurry in case the kids come by," Margo says, and everyone laughs again. Margo wonders why she's so damn funny, but the pot is starting to calm her, relaxing the muscles in her face. She takes a solid hit from the joint and then hands it to Sammy, who licks his fingers and tends to the burning tip. "It's worth the money," Tammi says and everyone nods in agreement. They smoke it down to the end and then wander back to the card table, fresh beers in hand.

Tommy deals the cards and everyone starts to sort their hands, focusing hard on the diamonds and clubs and spades and hearts, counting and recounting the numbers. "I don't know if I can get anything," Tammi says, "I can hardly read the cards." Margo notices Sammy catch Tommy's attention, motioning toward the two women. "Are you two cheating?" Margo asks, and Sammy and Tommy laugh yet again, but this time Margo admits that something about what she said, what exactly she can't say, is kind of funny.

"I was thinking, Tommy," Sammy says, "that maybe we could try that game I told you about." Tommy smiles and shakes his head, shuffling the cards in his hands.

"I don't think that'd be such a good idea," Tommy says, avoiding Margo's gaze. "Is this that kissing game, Sammy?" Tammi asks. "Every time we get high, you have to think of some new game." The last time they smoked pot, burning a pan of Jiffy Pop on purpose in order to cover up the smell so the children wouldn't notice, it wasn't too long before they were all arm wrestling, Tommy and Sammy shirtless, flexing their biceps. Tommy had beaten everyone, round after round after round of hands clasped together, straining against each other, and the next morning none of them could raise their right arms without grimacing, their heads aching, nothing quite making sense.

Margo didn't like being the only one who didn't know about this game. "Kissing?" she said. "Who kisses who?" Sammy and Tommy looked at each other, giggling, and Sammy said, "You kiss everybody, if the cards say so."

Kammi kisses Caleb, flicking her tongue against his teeth when he opens his mouth wide enough, when he needs to catch his breath. His stomach is cramping and he shifts from side to side to try and slide out from under Kammi, but she is holding him down. "I wanna get up," Caleb says, opening his eyes, pulling away from her kisses. Kammi looks annoyed but she rolls off of him and lets him sit up. He stares at Kammi, her face bright red in patches, her nose starting to run. "I don't want to play anymore," he says, and she shrugs her shoulders. "It's fun," she says. "It gets fun." She kicks her leg out at the crayons, scattering them in several directions and Caleb is immediately grateful for something to do, gathering them up and sorting them again, making sure each one is lined up perfectly.

Sammy explains the rules quickly, already dealing the cards as he speaks. At the same time, everyone turns over a single card and if any of the numbers match, those people have to kiss. "What if all four of us put down matching cards?" Tammi asks. "Then it'll be our lucky night," Sammy says and Margo feels her face burn red. "I'm not sure if I want to play," she says, but Tommy leans over and rubs her arm. "We'll only play until our show starts," he says, "Just a few hands."

Everyone flips over a card, a seven of hearts, a jack of clubs, a three of hearts, and a nine of diamonds. Margo sighs, relieved. "Huh," Tammi says. "This isn't as fun as you said it would be." They flip over four more cards, no matches. "Give it time," Sammy says. "We'll work out the kinks as we go along."

On the fourth hand, there is a match. Tommy has a five of clubs and Margo has a five of diamonds. They stand and lean over the corner of the table, their lips meeting. Tommy holds the kiss a little longer than Margo would like, Tammi and Sammy chuckling beside them. "Well," Tommy says, "this isn't so bad."

The very next hand, Tammi and Tommy match up, both aces. "Here we go," says Sammy. Tommy scratches the back of his neck and looks over at Margo, who nods. "It's the rules, I guess," she says.

Tommy and Tammi turn in their chairs to face each other, knees touching. Tammi kisses him, placing both of her hands on his shoulders, turning her head just slightly to the left, and then they pull away. Tommy touches the top of his index finger against his bottom lip, holds it there, and then places his hand back on his stack of cards. Sammy slowly claps his hands together in congratulations, pop, pop, pop, pop. "Now we're having fun," Sammy says and Tommy turns quickly to him. "It's just a game," he says and then looks over at Margo, who nods, her chin almost hitting her chest.

Caleb wants to go back into the closet, a fistful of crayons in his hand like a bouquet of flowers. Kammi shakes her head, her arms crossed against her chest. "It's my room," she says, "so I decide." Caleb ignores her, afraid of the games she will want to play instead, and so he crawls beneath the hung clothes and starts to draw a flock of birds, the letter M over and over in the sky. Behind him, the door clicks shut, the closet suddenly pitch black. He leans his shoulder against the door but Kammi will not let him out, has slid a chair under the doorknob. "Kammi?" he says. "Okay, I'm ready to come out." There is silence on the other side of the door, a faint wisp of light seeping under the doorframe like smoke. "Not yet," she says. "I'm thinking."
"It's dark," Caleb says, starting to whimper. He can hear the hiss of the vaporizer and then the click of Kammi's fingernails against the door, tapping a message he cannot understand. "You can come out," she says, "but you have to do whatever I say." He nods and then realizes that she can't see him so he whispers, "Okay." He hears the chair slide away from the door and then light spills into the closet and there is Kammi's smiling face, her arms outstretched, ready to hug him.

Two kisses later, a tentative, open-mouthed kiss between Margo and Tammi, both of them surprised by the softness of the other's lips, and another, quicker, kiss between Tammi and Tommy, Sammy is the only person who hasn't kissed anyone. "I thought up the damn game," he said. "I should get to kiss whoever I want." Margo touches the tips of her fingers on her final playing card, the dread seeping into her stomach at the prospect of a match with Sammy, the taste of his mouth. They turn over their last cards, and there is a match, a pair of tens, Sammy and Tommy. Everyone laughs at the pairing, the game over, nothing broken or disrupted.

"Pucker up," Tommy says and Sammy kills the rest of his beer, smashes the can against his head, crumpling the aluminum as if it was paper. Tammi starts to sweep all the cards into one pile, but Sammy claps his hand on the table. "Well," he says, "let's do it." Tommy raises both hands in surrender. "I forfeit," he says. "Game over." Sammy is no longer smiling, a bright red ring forming on his forehead from the beer can. "Rules is rules, Tommy." Tommy looks at Margo, who looks at Tammi, who looks at the cards on the table. "It's just a game," Tommy says. "Right," Sammy says, "It's just a game. So let's go." Tommy laughs, his voice breaking. "Sammy?" he says.

Margo watches Sammy's face, the tiny beads of perspiration on his upper lip. He doesn't blink, doesn't flinch. She looks over at the clock, five minutes past *Hee-Haw* and she points to the time. "*Hee-Haw*'s on," she says. "That's nice," Sammy answers, still looking at Tommy. "We'll watch it in just a second." Tommy, unsure of how to proceed or what to say to put an end to all of this, leans toward Sammy, his left eye twitching.

"Let's just go watch *Hee-Haw*, Sammy," Tammi says, her voice exasperated. A beat, silence, and then Sammy smiles, punches Tommy in the shoulder, hard, which makes Tommy wince. "You heard the ladies," Sammy says, "*Hee-Haw*'s on," and then he pushes away from the table and opens the fridge for another beer.

Caleb hands his pants to Kammi, who carefully folds them and places them on the bed, next to his sweater. He is standing beside her, clothed only in his underwear and socks and he thinks, for the first time, how strange it would be for the Sub-Mariner on land, walking into a store or on a crowded sidewalk, wearing nothing but a tiny pair of swimming trunks. Things are better underwater, he imagines.

Kammi dumps the loose pieces of a puzzle onto the floor. She takes off her own clothes and sits with Caleb while they start sorting pieces by color, looking for the border of the picture. Caleb keeps thinking that he hears his mother coming to the door, the sound of footsteps in the hallway, but no one comes and he cannot decide if he is relieved or distressed by this. While Kammi hums to herself, running her hands through the pieces of the puzzle, Caleb finds it hard to stop glancing over at her, the lines of her body so similar to his, the sameness almost reassuring him.

He connects two pieces, locking one into the other, and Kammi claps her hands, excited, and kisses him on the cheek, rubbing the tip of her nose against his face. He pulls away from her, but she curls her finger, commanding him to come closer. He leans forward and she kisses him again, on the lips. She tugs on his ear and then runs a finger along his right eyebrow, as if she is fascinated by each part of him. She throws her arms around his neck, squeezing him, and he pretends that he is drowning, sinking to the bottom of the ocean, and that the Sub-Mariner has swept him up in his arms, pulling him closer and closer to the surface, holding him so tightly that he cannot move. Kammi drags her fingers through his hair and he closes his eyes.

Kammi takes his hand and places it against her cheek, softly stroking the skin. Caleb tries to bend his mouth into a smile, afraid, and Kammi lets go of his hand. "Take off your underwear," she says and tugs at the elastic at his waist.

Caleb starts to shake, tears welling up and falling down his face. He squeezes the muscles of his face, trying to stop himself, but the tears keep coming. "I can't," he says and Kammi purses her lips as if she's tasted something sour, the sight of Caleb's tears, a little baby. He starts to take in gulps of air, sputtering, and she backs away from him, crawls under the bed so that all he can see are her fingers and her eyes, shining, unblinking, waiting for what's next.

"Buck Owens is a handsome man," Sammy says, gesturing toward the man on the screen, who is strumming a guitar and smiling. Once the song is over, the cameras switch to a couple of men in overalls, crouched behind a patch of corn. "You're drunk, Sammy," Tammi says. "You shouldn't talk when you get drunk."
Margo waits impatiently for the end of the show so that they can gather up their son and go home, the evening making her more and more tired. She doesn't know what to say anymore, has exhausted the words necessary to say what she is thinking, and so she sits quietly while the show goes through the motions, knee-slapping, banjo-playing, joke-telling fun.

Before they sat down to watch *Hee-Haw*, she nudged Tommy and told him they should leave soon but Tommy didn't seem to hear her, his eyes glassy, his face pink and splotchy. Sammy had been sitting sullenly beside her on the sofa, unnaturally quiet, until this comment about Buck Owens, and Margo again doesn't know what to say. She does not find Buck Owens particularly handsome, the garishness of his clothes, the unflattering haircut, but Sammy, now leaning forward, points again at the TV. "If I was gonna go queer, I'd go queer for Buck Owens," he says, and there is silence in the room, no response that anyone can think of. Sammy leans back on the sofa and tries to take a sip from his empty can of beer. "Out of beer," he says, but makes no motion to get more, simply holds the can in his hand. "Buck Owens," he says, softly, almost a whisper.

When Caleb, shivering from the cold, starts to put on his clothes, Kammi, still under the bed, says nothing. He buckles his pants and feels safe again, protected. He hides in the corner of the room, away from the bed so Kammi cannot see him, and crouches beside the vaporizer, the machine softly rattling and hissing, changing water into air like a magic trick.

"Come under the bed," Kammi says, but Caleb doesn't move. "One," she says, waiting a beat before she keeps going, "two...three..." but Caleb leans against the vaporizer as if to hide, the warmth radiating from the machine, the hissing in his ear like someone whispering, someone with a secret to tell. He will not go to her, and his mind flips through the possibilities of escape, of gaining the upper hand. "You better come right now," she says, and Caleb presses his hand against the open mouth of the vaporizer, the steam moving so quickly from the machine that it seems to pass through the skin and out the other side of his hand.

Pain travels up his arm, all the way to his teeth, which chatter violently. He thinks he hears someone calling his name but his head is buzzing. "What?" he says, "What?" and his hand is numb, and there is the smell of burning, and when he pulls his hand away, the skin slides off the palm of his hand like it was a wet sheet of paper. There are ragged pieces of flesh hanging off his hand and he frantically tears at them, trying to make the skin smooth again, uniform. Kammi comes out from under the bed and sees his hand, what is left of it, and screams, the sound so high it chokes itself out while her mouth is still open. Caleb stares at her mouth, the perfect O her lips make, and he holds his hand out to her, the mess he has made, and she screams again, even louder.

When Margo reaches the door of Kammi's room, she finds the two children, Kammi nearly naked, her chest bare, and her son, standing quietly in the corner of the room, holding his hand out as if waiting for his palm to be read. Before she can ask what is going on, she smells burning flesh, the sharp scent making her flinch, and she finally notices Caleb's hand, the top layer of skin evaporated, burned away. "He touched the steam," Kammi says. "I didn't tell him to do it."

Tommy, who is now standing behind Margo and has sobered up just from contact with the situation at hand, pushes past his wife, who cannot move, and scoops up Caleb, running back into the hallway with his son in his arms. "Do we call the ambulance?" Tammi asks. "What do we do?" Tommy grabs the keys off the counter and yells for

Margo, who is still standing in the room, staring at Kammi, shirtless, her nose running. "Dammit, Margo," Tommy shouts. "C'mon." Sammy is still sitting on the sofa, drunk, oblivious to the activity. "You want us to come with?" he asks, but Tommy is already running across the street, toward the car in the driveway.

Tammi stands beside Margo and places her hand on her shoulder. "You should go, honey," she says. "Tommy's leaving." Margo, her hands clenching and unclenching like spasms, a rush of anger burning her ears, steps toward Kammi. "What happened, Kammi? What happened to Caleb?" Kammi backs away from her and whimpers, "It wasn't my fault." Tammi kneels beside her daughter and pulls a shirt over her head. "You should probably go now, Margo," Tammi says. Margo turns without a word and walks into the living room. Sammy raises his hand as she opens the front door. "See you next week?" he asks.

Standing in the doorway, her anger undiffused and expanding, Margo listens to the sound of the car horn, frantic and irregular. She wants to punch Sammy in the face, to set the entire house on fire, but then she remembers her son, the hand open and trembling. She steps outside, the shock of cold on her skin, and feels her anger harden, turning from a gas into a solid, heavy in her chest. She can feel it as she breathes, but she keeps running toward the car, the engine idling and then revving, the hi-beams blinding her, illuminating the snow as it falls.

The car moves slowly, the roads slick with snow, just starting to freeze. In the backseat, Caleb lays his head on his mother's lap. She holds his burned hand away from him to keep him from touching it, something he wants to do very badly. He can't feel anything. He stares at his hand, the skin glistening and wet, and he knows it is a part of him, but he cannot locate it. It is his hand and no one else's, right in front of his face, and yet hidden from him. The car bumps along the road, his mother holding him, the snow whipping against the windows, and Caleb falls asleep before he can feel the part of him that is damaged.

*Kevin Wilson is the author of the collection, Tunneling to the Center of the Earth (Ecco/Harper Perennial, 2009), which received an Alex Award from the American Library Association and the Shirley Jackson Award, and a novel, The Family Fang (Ecco, 2011). wilsonkevin.com*

## ABOUT JOYLAND

Joyland is an online literary magazine that curates fiction regionally. We've chosen several editors to select and post stories by authors connected to locales across North America every week. Visit us at joylandmagazine.com

Made in the USA
Charleston, SC
05 February 2012